CALLED TO BE A CHAMPION

THE ULTIMATE BIBLE-BASED PLAYBOOK FOR FEMALE ATHLETES

FROM: _____

TO: _____

DATE: _____

NOTE: _____

Disclaimer and Legal Notice

PRAISE

Maya W., High School Senior and Multi-Sport Athlete

Most devotionals feel like they were written by people who have never actually broken a sweat. This one is different. It actually gets what it is like to deal with an ACL tear, get stuck on the bench, or feel like trash because your stats were low. I wrote "Child of God" on my wrist tape after one of the readings, and it completely changed my headspace during games. I am playing more aggressive, and I am not as scared to make mistakes because my worth is not riding on one play anymore. It also helped me during recruiting season, especially on the days when I felt behind or overlooked, and made me enjoy my sport again. It is the first thing I grab in the morning before I head to the weight room.

Emily S., Athlete Mom

I bought this for my daughter and ended up reading it too. It speaks to the pressure, the bench, the injuries, and the identity stuff in a way that feels honest, and it points back to Jesus without being cheesy or preachy. The devotionals are short, practical, and easy to keep up with during a busy season. It is the kind of book that gives you language for conversations you have been trying to have. This is a gift I will keep buying for the athletes in our family.

David P., Father of an All-State Volleyball Player

As a dad, watching my daughter struggle under the weight of perfectionism was heartbreaking. We started reading this on our morning car rides to tournaments, just a few pages at a time, and it became something we both looked forward to. It speaks directly to the "Instagram versus real life" pressure and the expectations girls feel to look a certain way, even while they are training hard. My daughter used to see her strength as a flaw. After reading the Strong is Beautiful devotional, she started seeing her muscles as God-given tools for her mission. If you have a daughter in sports, this is not just a book. It is a steady voice when the world gets loud.

Coach Elena R., Head Varsity Soccer Coach, Florida

In over fifteen years of coaching young women, I have learned the biggest battles are not won on the field. They are won in the mind and in the heart. I will never forget sitting with one of my starters after a playoff loss. She had missed a penalty kick and could barely look up because she thought she had let everyone down. Called to Be a Champion for Girls has been the steady voice my athletes need in moments like that. It names the performance trap for what it is and anchors their value in Christ, not in minutes, stats, or the scoreboard. The practice sections are especially strong. We started using the gratitude prompts and identity statements as part of our pre-game rhythm, and it changed the tone in our locker room. There is more calm, more courage, and more joy. This book does not just help them compete better. It helps them become more resilient, confident young women.

Pastor Mike J., Collegiate Ministry Leader and Former D1 Athlete

I wish I had this playbook when I was competing in college. It connects the locker room and the altar with remarkable clarity. The devotionals on injury and feeling unseen on the bench are deeply empathetic and biblically grounded. It reminds our female athletes that their sport is a platform, not a pedestal. We use these readings to launch our small groups, and the conversations they spark are some of the most honest I have ever heard, real athletes talking about real pressure, real fear, and real faith. It is short, punchy, and spiritually powerful long after the final whistle.

00

INTRODUCTION

You are a girl with a big dream and a heart full of fire.

Imagine the sun on your face and the wind in your hair as you run. Picture the roar of the crowd when you score. Think about the high-fives from your teammates and the pure joy of playing the sport you love. You were made for this. You were created to move, to compete, and to shine.

But sometimes the lights go out.

Sometimes you strike out with the bases loaded. You feel the sting of tears behind your goggles. You look at your phone and see everyone else's "perfect" life while you feel like a failure. Maybe you are sitting on the bench wishing you were invisible. Or maybe you are staring at a heavy brace on your knee wondering if you will ever be the same again.

The world tells you that you are only as good as your last game. It says you have to be perfect to be loved. It says your stats are who you are.

That is where the world is wrong. And that is why Jesus is the answer.

Sydney McLaughlin-Levrone is the fastest woman to ever run the hurdles. But she does not find her worth in her gold medals. She finds her peace in the Bible. She knows that even if she never ran another race, God would still call her His daughter.

Caitlin Clark became a basketball legend by practicing in the dark when no one was watching. But she knows that her talent is a gift from above. She plays with joy because she knows her true reward is not a trophy. It is the love of her Creator.

Simone Biles showed the world that it is okay to be brave and say when you are not okay. She reminds us that our souls are more important than our gymnastics routines. She trusts that God holds her heart even when she is not flying through the air.

Coco Gauff wins big titles on the tennis court and then immediately drops to her knees to pray. She wants you to know that the greatest win is knowing Jesus. He is the one who calms her nerves when the pressure is at its highest.

This book is your secret playbook. It is a warm hug and a pep talk from a sister who has been there. Each page is a reminder that you are loved for who you are, not just for how you play.

You will learn that you are a daughter of the King. This means you never have to play for a scoreboard again.

You will find out that your body is a gift. Your muscles and your strength were designed by the Master Architect.

You will discover how to be a leader. You can change the energy of your whole team just by being kind.

You will see that mistakes are just lessons. God uses every "fail" to build your character into something beautiful.

So grab your sneakers and take a deep breath. You are not alone in the locker room or on the field. The King of the Universe is your ultimate Coach. He is cheering for you in the quiet moments and holding you in the hard ones.

You are called to be a champion. Not because of what you do, but because of whose you are.

Turn the page. Your beautiful journey starts right now.

HOW TO USE YOUR PLAYBOOK

1. One Minute Just for You

Read one page every day. It only takes a minute. You can read it while you eat breakfast or right before you put on your cleats.

2. Talk to Your Best Friend

The prayers at the end of each page are just short talks with Jesus. He loves to hear your voice. Tell Him about your big goals and your scary fears.

3. Do the Practice

Every day has a small action step. It might be writing a note to a teammate or saying something kind to yourself in the mirror. These small reps build a strong heart.

4. Do Not Worry About Being Perfect

If you miss a day, do not sweat it. Just start again today. God's grace is like a fresh start every single morning.

5. Share the Love

If a page really helps you, tell a friend about it. Champions help other people grow. You can even read one out loud with your mom or your coach. The clock is starting and the game is on. But remember, you have already won because Jesus is on your side.

You are brave. You are strong. You are His.

TABLE OF CONTENTS

CHAPTER 5: LOVING MY TEAMMATES

CHAPTER 6: CHARACTER UNDER PRESSURE

BONUSES

If you are a teen, please ask your parent to sign up for the bonuses.

Want to remember the verses? Or test yourself whenever you want on your phone and know which verse means what?

We made a simple flashcards for you on Quizlet.com.

We made 50 fun flashcards with hints and scripture.

And we made 20 fun ones for the parents.

Scan this QR code and get access today!

Called to be Christian Parents Community

Stop navigating the high-pressure, toxic sports and school culture alone.

Join a our community of Christian parents dedicated to building rooted reens who are even stronger in their faith.

What's Inside the Community:

» Safe Community: Connect with parents who value character over the scoreboard.

» Use the map to connect to other Christian parents close to you who also bought our books and joined.

» Get all of our next books sent to you for free as an advanced reviewer.

» Custom Worship Song: A professional anthem featuring your teens name & scripture of your choice ($250 Value!)

» Recruiting & Scholarship Kit: Clear steps to the next level without the stress.

» More bonuses and materials added continously!

Scan the QR code to Join us.

CHAPTER 1:
WHO I AM

01
MY WORTH VS. MY STATS

"However, do not rejoice that the spirits submit to you, but rejoice that your names are written in heaven." (Luke 10:20)

The stadium roars. The lights are blinding. Then, sudden silence. A stretcher carries Mallory Swanson off the field right before the World Cup. She was the top scorer, the star, the unstoppable force. In an instant, the stats column hit zero. Sitting in rehab, watching her team play without her, the silence was loud. She had to ask herself a hard question. Who is she without the jersey? Mallory realized that soccer is just what she does, not who she is. It is easy to feel like a failure when you strike out, drop the ball, or get benched. You feel your value drop with your batting average. But Jesus does not love you for your hat tricks or personal bests. He loves you because you are His. When the game is taken away, you remain. You are not a stat sheet. You are a daughter of the King. Play freely because your worth is already secured in Heaven, not on the scoreboard. You can risk everything on the field because you have nothing to lose in your soul. Your name is carved in stone, even if your stats are erased.

Prayer:

Lord, remind me I am loved for who I am, not how I play. My name is written in Heaven. Amen.

Practice:

Write "Child of God" on your wrist tape or shoe. Look at it when you make a mistake today.

02

INSTAGRAM VS. REAL LIFE

"The Lord does not look at the things people look at... The Lord looks at the heart." (1 Samuel 16:7)

The clock flashes a world record. Sydney McLaughlin-Levrone sits on the track, hair perfect, smile wide. Millions like the photo on Instagram. It looks effortless. But the screen does not show the anxiety attacks, the crying in the locker room, or the lonely 5 AM sprints in the rain. Social media shows the highlight reel, but God sees the behind the scenes footage. Sydney constantly reminds fans that the internet is not real life. Only Jesus offers a solid foundation. You scroll through feeds seeing perfect abs, perfect teams, and gold medals, feeling like you are failing. Stop comparing your raw footage to their edited movie. God looks past the filters and sees your heart. He sees your effort when no one is watching. That is where real champions are made. He is not impressed by your follower count; He is captivated by your faithfulness. Build a life that feels good on the inside, not just one that looks good on the outside. When you seek His approval, the likes on a screen stop mattering so much.

Prayer:

God, help me stop comparing my life to screens. Help me see myself through Your eyes, not likes. Amen.

Practice:

Unfollow one account that makes you feel bad about yourself. Replace scrolling with five minutes of silence.

03

LOVED EVEN WHEN I LOSE

"For I am convinced that neither death nor life... nor anything else in all creation, will be able to separate us from the love of God." (Romans 8:38-39)

The final ball hits the floor. The other team screams in victory. Jordan Larson stands under the net, the weight of the loss heavy on her shoulders. But Jordan faced a darker valley than losing a gold medal match. She lost her mom to cancer. In that deep grief, volleyball wins could not fix the pain, and volleyball losses could not make it worse. She realized that God's love is the only constant thing in the universe. A championship trophy collects dust. A bad game is forgotten in a week. But His love never quits on you. When you miss the game winning shot, He is there. When you feel alone on the bus ride home, He is there. Your performance changes daily, but His love is locked in forever. You do not have to earn His affection with a win. It is already yours. This truth frees you from the crushing pressure to perform. You can play hard, not to earn love, but because you are already loved. Win or lose, your status as His beloved daughter never changes.

Prayer:

Father, thank You that winning does not make You love me more, and losing does not make You love me less. Amen.

Practice:

After your next game or practice, say out loud, "Win or lose, I am fully loved."

04

INVISIBLE ON THE BENCH

"On the contrary, those parts of the body that seem to be weaker are indispensable." (1 Corinthians 12:22)

The buzzer sounds. The starters high five at center court. You are sitting on the bench, warm up shirt still on, sweating only from nerves. It feels humiliating. You worked just as hard in practice. Kayla Alexander knows this grind in the WNBA. Sometimes she starts, sometimes she cheers. It is easy to feel invisible or useless when you aren't scoring points. But Scripture says the parts of the body that seem weaker are actually necessary. A team collapses without the bench pushing the starters in practice. The culture says you only matter if you are the MVP. God says you matter because you are part of the body. Your attitude on the sideline can shift the energy of the whole game. A quiet leader on the bench is often more powerful than a loud star on the court. Be the best teammate, loud and proud, right where you are planted. Your value is not in your minutes played, but in the spirit you bring. God sees your faithfulness in the shadows just as clearly as He sees the spotlight.

Prayer:

Jesus, help me serve my team with joy, whether I play zero minutes or the whole game. I matter. Amen.

Practice:

High five every single teammate today. Compliment someone who plays the same position as you.

05
HATING HOW I LOOK

"I praise you because I am fearfully and wonderfully made; your works are wonderful, I know that full well." (Psalm 139:14)

Cameras flash. Critics whisper. They called Serena Williams too manly. They said her arms were too big and her shape was wrong for tennis. It would have been easy to hide, to wear long sleeves, to shrink into the background. Instead, Serena served aces at 120 miles per hour. She realized her thick legs were engines for power. Her strong arms were weapons for victory. God designed your body specifically for your mission. Maybe you have broad shoulders to swim fast, or thick thighs to squat heavy. That is not a flaw. That is a feature. Stop wishing for a runway model body. You are an athlete. Your body is an instrument, not an ornament. Thank God for the power He packed into your frame and use it to glorify Him. Own your design. It was crafted by the Master Architect to do great things. When you look in the mirror, do not look for what is wrong. Look for the power God gave you to run, jump, and compete. Strong is beautiful because God made it.

Prayer:

Lord, thank You for this strong body. Help me see my muscles as gifts, not flaws. I am wonderfully made. Amen.

Practice:

Look in the mirror. Find the body part you criticize most. Thank God for what it helps you do in your sport.

06
THE SCHOLARSHIP IDOL

"But seek first his kingdom and his righteousness, and all these things will be given to you as well." (Matthew 6:33)

The net cuts. The confetti falls. Maya Moore was the queen of basketball. Two NCAA titles, four WNBA championships, Olympic gold. She had every scout, sponsor, and scholarship offer imaginable. Then, she walked away. She stopped playing at the peak of her career to fight for a man wrongly imprisoned. The world was shocked. Why give up the glory? Maya knew that basketball was a great job, but it was a terrible god. We often crush ourselves chasing the scholarship, thinking it will save us. We stress over emails to coaches and stats. But accolades are temporary. Justice and love are eternal. Chase the Kingdom first. The right doors for college will open if you keep your priorities straight. Your sport is your platform, not your savior. Release the tight grip on your future and watch how God leads you when your hands are open. When you stop worshiping the scholarship, you can actually enjoy the game again. Trust that God's plan for your future is better than your stress about it.

Prayer:

God, I surrender my future. I trust You with college and scholarships. I seek You first. Handle the rest. Amen.

Practice:

Do not check your recruiting profile or email for 24 hours. Spend that time reading one chapter of Matthew.

07
COACH'S VOICE VS. GOD'S

"We must obey God rather than human beings!" (Acts 5:29)

The dugout is loud. The coach is screaming. The pressure to fit in, to talk trash, or to cut corners feels heavy. In softball culture, you do what the coach says, no matter what. Janie Reed, USA Olympian, faced moments where the team culture clashed with her faith. It is scary to stand out. It is terrifying to be the only one not laughing at the dirty joke or the gossip. But Janie learned to tune her ear to a higher frequency. A coach determines your playing time, but God determines your path. Respect your coach, but never let them take the throne of your heart. If the locker room asks you to compromise who you are, stand firm. Quiet confidence in God speaks louder than screaming instructions. Be respectful, but be holy. Your character will outlast your season. You might feel alone in that moment, but you are standing with the King of Kings. Do not trade your integrity for a starting spot. Listen to the voice of truth above the noise of the crowd.

Prayer:

Father, give me the courage to stand for truth even when my voice shakes. You are my ultimate Coach. Amen.

Practice:

If gossip starts in the locker room today, change the subject or walk away. Be the difference.

08

INJURED AND FEELING USELESS

"Therefore we do not lose heart. Though outwardly we are wasting away, yet inwardly we are being renewed day by day." (2 Corinthians 4:16)

The pop was loud. The pain was sharp. Paige Bueckers, the college basketball sensation, lay on the court holding her knee. ACL tear. Season over. For months, she was on crutches, watching others play the game she loved. It felt like her purpose was stripped away. The silence of rehab is harder than the noise of the game. But Paige posted a message: "I am a living testimony." She realized her spirit did not have an ACL. Her body was broken, but her inner self could still grow stronger. Injury is not a pause button on your life. It is a pivot. You can train your mind, encourage your teammates, and deepen your prayer life. Your body might be wasting away on the couch, but your spirit can be renewed every single morning. You are still useful to God, even on crutches. Do not waste your waiting. Use this time to build a mental toughness that no injury can touch. Your comeback story starts in the quiet moments with God, long before you step back on the court.

Prayer:

Healer, comfort my heart when my body hurts. Renew my spirit today. Show me my purpose beyond the game. Amen.

Practice:

If you are injured, visualize your perfect game for 10 minutes. If healthy, send a text to an injured teammate.

A Quick Blessing

Your feedback is a true blessing!

If this book has encouraged you or helped you feel less alone, would you leave a quick review?

Even one sentence makes a huge difference and takes just a minute. As a small author, your feedback not only lifts my heart... it also helps other children of God find the support and hope they need.

Thank you for being part of this journey!

Scan this QR code with your phone to go to the review page

Or

Go to your orders, find the book and click

"Write a product review"

Thank you <3

09

STRONG IS BEAUTIFUL

"She sets about her work vigorously; her arms are strong for her tasks." (Proverbs 31:17)

The barbell bends. The weights clang against the floor. Elana Meyers Taylor lifts massive weight to push a heavy bobsled down an icy track. She does not look like a fragile doll. She looks like a warrior. The world often tells girls to be small, to take up less space. But the Proverbs 31 woman clothes herself with strength. She girds her arms for the task. Elana embraced her power because her sport demanded it. Do not be afraid of the weight room. Do not fear getting "bulky." Strength is functional. Strength protects you from injury. Strength allows you to dominate the paint, drive the ball, and sprint the final leg. God gave you muscles to use them. Be proud of what your body can lift. Strong is not just beautiful. It is biblical. Step up to the bar and lift with gratitude. Do not shrink yourself to fit a worldly standard. Expand yourself to fit God's calling. Your power is a testimony to His design. Lift heavy, run fast, and give Him the glory.

Prayer:

God, thank You for the strength in my veins. Help me train hard and love the power You gave me. Amen.

Practice:

Add 2.5 or 5 pounds to your lift today, or do one extra pushup. Celebrate your physical power.

10
PERFECTIONISM IS CRUSHING ME

"My grace is sufficient for you, for my power is made perfect in weakness."
(2 Corinthians 12:9)

The toes must be pointed. The landing must be stuck. The smile must be fake. Laurie Hernandez grew up in the strict world of gymnastics where a 9.9 is a failure. The pressure to be perfect nearly crushed her spirit. She was an Olympian, but she was exhausted. She had to learn to find the joy again. She realized that grace covers the wobbles. Jesus said His power is made perfect in weakness, not in our 10.0 routines. You do not have to be a robot. You are allowed to have a bad practice. You are allowed to fall off the beam. Perfectionism is a heavy chain; grace is wings. Let go of the need to be flawless. Embrace the freedom of doing your best and letting God handle the rest. Joy is a better fuel than fear. When you realize that God loves you even when you stumble, the fear of failure evaporates. You can fly through the air with a genuine smile, knowing that your identity is safe in His hands, no matter how you land.

Prayer:

Jesus, I release the heavy burden of being perfect. I accept Your grace. I will play with joy today. Amen.

Practice:

Make a mistake in practice? Laugh it off. Literally laugh. Then try again. Break the tension with joy.

11

ADDICTED TO APPLAUSE

Am I now trying to win the approval of human beings, or of God? If I were still trying to please people, I would not be a servant of Christ. (Galatians 1:10)

The water in the Olympic pool is still and blue before the splash. Tatjana Smith, the legendary South African swimmer, dives into the silence. When she touches the wall and sees the number one, the arena explodes. Fans scream her name and cameras flash like tiny stars. It feels amazing to be loved by the world, but Tatjana knows a secret. If you live for their cheers, you will die by their silence. She decided long ago that her swimming is a private conversation between her and God. Even when she broke world records, she whispered that she was "running for an audience of one." You might feel the same pressure when you look at your likes on social media or wait for your coach to say "good job." It is easy to become a slave to what people think. Galatians 1:10 reminds us that we serve a King, not a crowd. When you play for Him, you are already enough. You can swim, run, or jump with total freedom because His love never moves.

Prayer

Lord, help me focus on Your smile today. I choose to play for You alone and ignore the noise. Amen.

Practice

List three people whose opinions matter too much. Today, perform only for God. How does that feel?

12
HER WIN IS NOT MY LOSS

Rejoice with those who rejoice; mourn with those who mourn. (Romans 12:15)

The track is hot and the stakes are higher. Sydney McLaughlin-Levrone just crossed the finish line in a blur of speed, breaking the world record again. But instead of dancing alone, she turns around immediately. She finds Dalilah Muhammad, her toughest rival, and pulls her into a deep hug. There is no bitterness or jealousy in her eyes. Sydney knows that Dalilah's greatness actually pushed her to be better. In the world of track and field, people expect runners to be enemies. Sydney shows us something different. She follows Romans 12:15 by celebrating her teammate and her competitor. For a teen athlete, it is hard when a friend gets the starting spot or the MVP trophy. You might feel like their success makes you look small. But God says there is enough room for everyone to shine. When you celebrate a teammate, you kill the monster of envy. You realize that her gold medal does not make your silver any less bright.

Prayer

Jesus, take away my jealousy. Help me be truly happy for my teammates when they succeed and win big. Amen.

Practice

Congratulate a rival or teammate today on something they did well. Be specific and be very kind.

13
GOD MADE ME FAST

Each of you should use whatever gift you have received to serve others, as faithful stewards of God's grace. (1 Peter 4:10)

Rain pours down on the purple track in Paris, but Julien Alfred is a bolt of lightning. The sprinter from St. Lucia flies across the pavement to win her country's first Olympic medal. She is the fastest woman in the world, yet her heart is full of quiet gratitude. Julien does not walk around acting like she invented her own speed. She says clearly that God gave her the gift, and she is simply the one who uses it. This perspective changes everything. When you realize your talent is a loan from God, you stop being arrogant and start being thankful. Whether you are great at soccer, volleyball, or cross country, that spark inside you was placed there by your Creator. 1 Peter 4:10 tells us we are just managers of God's grace. This takes the heavy pressure off your shoulders. You do not have to "be" the best; you just have to "use" what He gave you. When you compete, you are showing off His beautiful work to the world.

Prayer

Lord, thank You for the specific talents You gave me. I use my body to give You glory today. Amen.

Practice

What is one specific physical gift God gave you? Use it today with a heart full of gratitude.

14
EMPTY WITHOUT A SEASON

There is a time for everything, and a season for every activity under the heavens. (Ecclesiastes 3:1)

Lauren Holiday stood in the middle of a roaring stadium, clutching a World Cup trophy. She was at the very top of the soccer world, yet she decided to walk away. She retired while she was still a superstar because she knew her season on the field was ending. For many athletes, the thought of hanging up the jersey is terrifying. They wonder who they are if they aren't "the soccer girl" or "the star point guard." Lauren found peace because her identity was not built on grass and goals. She knew she was a wife, a mother, and most importantly, a believer. Ecclesiastes 3:1 tells us that life moves in cycles. There is a time to compete and a time to rest. If you get injured or the season ends, you might feel empty. But remember that you are more than your stats. Your value does not drop when the scoreboard turns off. God loves you just as much in the off-season as He does when you are winning championships.

Prayer

Father, remind me that my identity is in You, not my sport. I trust You with every new season. Amen.

Practice

Write down three things you love about yourself that have nothing to do with sports or your performance.

"*Get up, you're not done yet.*"

CHAPTER 2: PEACE IN THE STORM

15
MY STOMACH IS IN KNOTS

"Do not be anxious about anything, but in every situation, by prayer and petition, with thanksgiving, present your requests to God. And the peace of God… will guard your hearts." — Philippians 4:6-7

The pool deck is chaotic. The smell of chlorine stings your nose and the crowd noise is a deafening roar. Katie Ledecky is the greatest swimmer in history, yet even she battles nerves. Before she steps onto the block to race, she does something specific. She doesn't just stretch. She whispers a "Hail Mary" prayer. Katie uses that moment to hand her nerves over to God. She knows that the butterflies in her stomach are just energy looking for a place to go. Instead of letting that energy turn into panic, she turns it into power through prayer. When you stand at the starting line, or wait for the whistle, your stomach might feel like it is doing flips. That is okay. It means you are ready to care. But do not carry the heavy weight of worry. Do what Katie does. Pause. Whisper to God. Tell Him you are nervous. Then, visualize those knots untying and turning into fuel. You are not alone in the water. God is your peace when the pressure gets loud.

Prayer:

God, take these knots in my stomach. Turn my nervousness into strength and help me swim with a calm heart. Amen.

Practice:

When you feel butterflies today, say "God, I give this energy to You" and take a deep breath.

16

THE "WHAT IF" SPIRAL

"Therefore do not worry about tomorrow, for tomorrow will worry about itself. Each day has enough trouble of its own." — Matthew 6:34

Keni Harrison stood on the track, heartbroken. It was 2016 and the American hurdler had just missed the Olympic team. The "what ifs" started screaming in her head. What if I am not good enough? What if I never get another chance? It is easy to spiral when things go wrong. But Keni refused to stay in the dark. She went back to work. Just weeks later, she didn't just win a race; she smashed the world record. She learned that looking at the scary future trips you up. You have to look at the hurdle right in front of you. When you make a mistake in a game, your brain wants to fast forward to the loss. Stop. Matthew 6:34 tells us to stay in today. God gives you strength for this play, this inning, this second. You cannot control the scoreboard five minutes from now. You can only control your effort right now. Stop asking "what if" and start saying "what now." Be where your feet are.

Prayer:

Lord, silence the "what ifs" in my head. Help me focus entirely on this moment and trust You with my future. Amen.

Practice:

Catch yourself worrying about the future. Snap a rubber band on your wrist or clap your hands to reset.

17

PLAYING FOR AUDIENCE OF ONE

"Whatever you do, work at it with all your heart, as working for the Lord, not for human masters." — Colossians 3:23

The high jump bar sits impossibly high. The stadium watches, waiting for a failure. Nicola Olyslagers, an Australian high jumper, stands tall. She grabs a marker and writes on her wrist. She isn't checking her stats or looking at her coach's frowning face. She jumps for an Audience of One. Nicola realized that performing for people is exhausting. You worry about what your teammates think, what the crowd thinks, or what the scouts think. That pressure is like wearing a backpack full of rocks. When Nicola decided she was jumping just to bring God joy, the weight fell off. She jumps higher because she feels lighter. You can do this too. When you step on the court, imagine the stands are empty except for Jesus. He is not judging you; He is delighting in the talent He gave you. Play hard, sweat, and smile. You are not there to impress the world. You are there to say "Thank you" to your Creator with your effort.

Prayer:

Jesus, I play for You alone. Help me ignore the crowd and find joy in using the gifts You gave me. Amen.

Practice:

Draw a small cross or heart on your wrist or shoe. Let it remind you who you really play for.

18

TERRIFIED I WILL CHOKE

"So do not fear, for I am with you; do not be dismayed, for I am your God. I will strengthen you and help you." — Isaiah 41:10

Standing ten meters above the pool, the water looks like concrete. Andrea Spendolini-Sirieix, a champion diver from Great Britain, knows fear. She faced the "twisties," a terrifying mental block where her body wouldn't listen to her brain in mid-air. She was scared she would get hurt. She was scared she would choke. Instead of quitting, she leaned on Isaiah 41:10. She realized that fear makes you freeze, but faith makes you fly. Andrea memorized scripture to drown out the voice of fear. When you are staring down a fast pitcher or preparing for a balance beam routine, terror tries to shrink you. It whispers that you will fail. Talk back to it. God says, "I will hold you." You do not have to be fearless to be brave. You just have to trust that God is standing right there on the platform with you. Take the breath. Trust your training. God is your spotter. He will not let you go. You are safe in His grip.

Prayer:

Father, when fear tries to freeze me, remind me You are here. Give me courage to move even when I am scared. Amen.

Practice:

Memorize "I will strengthen you." Repeat it three times right before you attempt the scary skill or play today.

19

I CAN'T SLEEP TONIGHT

"In peace I will lie down and sleep, for you alone, Lord, make me dwell in safety." — Psalm 4:8

The night before the big game is brutal. The room is dark, but your mind is running sprints. Cat Osterman, a softball legend, knows this struggle. With gold medals on the line, the pressure to be perfect kept her mind racing. She replayed pitches and analyzed batters while staring at the ceiling. Then she learned the secret of Psalm 4:8. Sleep is an act of trust. When you stay awake worrying, you are trying to control tomorrow. Cat learned to mentally hand the ball to God before closing her eyes. She realized the world keeps spinning even when she isn't managing it. You need rest to perform. Lying awake stressing drains your battery before the game even starts. Visualize yourself packing up all your worries about the game into a box. Imagine handing that box to Jesus. He stays awake so you do not have to. Close your eyes. Your strength for tomorrow comes from resting in Him tonight. Let go and let God hold the night.

Prayer:

Lord, my mind is racing. I give tomorrow's game to You. Help me sleep in peace knowing You are in control. Amen.

Practice:

No screens 30 minutes before bed. Visualize handing your jersey to Jesus, trusting Him to handle the outcome tomorrow.

20
VISUALIZING GOD ON THE FIELD

"I keep my eyes always on the Lord. With him at my right hand, I will not be shaken." — Psalm 16:8

Skate parks are loud, gritty, and full of concrete. It is easy to feel small. Rayssa Leal, the Brazilian skateboarding phenomenon, brings a secret weapon to the park. It isn't a new board. It is vision. Before she drops in to do tricks that defy gravity, she prays with her dad. She visualizes peace in the middle of a war zone. Rayssa pictures God right there with her. Not up in the clouds, but at her right hand. When you compete, the opponent feels big and the problem feels huge. Change your view. Use your imagination to see Jesus standing on the court next to you. If the Creator of the universe is your teammate, what is there to be shaken by? It changes how you stand. You stop looking at the scoreboard with panic and start looking at the challenge with confidence. He is closer than your jersey. Keep your eyes on Him, and your feet will stay steady.

Prayer:

God, open my eyes to see You on the field with me. Let Your presence make me brave and steady today. Amen.

Practice:

Before the whistle blows, close your eyes for two seconds and picture Jesus standing right next to you, ready to play.

21
FLUSH THE MISTAKE

"Forgetting what is behind and straining toward what is ahead." — Philippians 3:13

Gymnastics is brutal. One wobble, one step out of bounds, and your score drops. Grace McCallum knows this pressure. In a sport where perfection is the goal, a mistake can ruin your whole mood. But Grace has a rule: short memory. She prays to reset. She treats a mistake like a toilet—she flushes it. If she dwells on the balance beam fall, she will mess up the floor routine too. You cannot change the turnover you just made. You cannot unsink the missed shot. Replaying it in your head only steals your focus from the next play. Be like Grace. Acknowledge the mess up, learn from it in one second, and then flush it. It is gone. The most important play in sports is always the next one. God's mercies are new every morning, and in sports, they are new every possession. Don't carry dead weight. Flush it. Move on. Win the next moment. Your potential is ahead of you, not behind you.

Prayer:

Lord, help me forgive myself for mistakes instantly. I choose to forget what is behind and focus on the next play. Amen.

Practice:

Create a physical "flush" motion with your hand. Use it in practice immediately after you mess up to signal a reset.

22
STRESS MEANS I CARE

"Cast all your anxiety on him because he cares for you." — 1 Peter 5:7

The sand is hot and the stakes are high. Kerri Walsh Jennings is a beach volleyball icon, but she isn't a robot. She feels stress. Her heart pounds just like yours. But Kerri views stress differently. She realized that stress just means she cares about the outcome. It means she loves the game. She doesn't run from the feeling; she leans on her "safety net." She casts the worry part to God. Anxiety tells you that you aren't ready. Faith tells you that God is with you. When your palms sweat, don't hate it. It is your body preparing you to fight. Take the fear part—the part that says "I'm going to fail"—and throw it to God. Keep the adrenaline. Use the energy to chase the ball, to run faster, to jump higher. God can handle your heavy fears. You just handle the game. Let stress be your battery, not your cage. Use the rush to be great.

Prayer:

Father, I cast my heavy anxiety to You. Thank You for this energy. Help me use it to play hard and free. Amen.

Practice:

When you feel stressed, say out loud: "This means I care, and God's got me." Then hustle harder.

23
STOP OVERTHINKING

"Trust in the Lord with all your heart and lean not on your own understanding." — Proverbs 3:5

Tennis is lonely. You are out there by yourself, and your brain can be your worst enemy. Shelby Rogers knows the trap of overthinking. She used to analyze every bad bounce, every missed swing, dissecting it until she was paralyzed. She realized she was leaning on her own understanding, and it was breaking her game. She started using scripture to quiet her brain. She had to stop being a scientist and start being an athlete. When you overthink, you move slow. You second-guess your instincts. You wonder if your form is right instead of just reacting. Stop it. You practiced the drills. You put in the work. Now, trust God and trust your gut. Your body knows what to do. Turn off the analysis. Turn on the trust. Play free. God guides your steps, so you don't have to micromanage every single one of them. Your best game happens when your mind is quiet and your heart is trusting.

Prayer:

Lord, quiet my busy mind. Help me stop analyzing and start trusting. I lean on You, not my own overthinking. Amen.

Practice:

If you catch yourself analyzing during a game, pick a focal point (like the rim or net) and just stare until your mind clears.

24
QUIET IN THE CHAOS

"The Lord will fight for you; you need only to be still." — Exodus 14:14

Caitlin Clark has changed basketball. But with fame comes noise. Fans scream, critics talk, and cameras flash. How does she shoot from the logo with ice in her veins? She finds quiet in the chaos. She knows who she is, so the noise doesn't shake her. The world of sports is loud. Your locker room might be full of drama. Social media is full of opinions. If you listen to it all, you will drown. You need a quiet center. Exodus says you need only to be still. This doesn't mean standing still on the court. It means being still in your soul. It means knowing God is fighting your battles, so you don't have to prove yourself to the haters. You just have to play. Let the crowd yell. Let the other team talk trash. You stay locked in. Your confidence comes from a quiet place that noise cannot touch. God is your defense and your shield. Let Him handle the critics.

Prayer:

God, block out the noise. Keep my heart still and confident in You, even when everything around me is loud and chaotic. Amen.

Practice:

Find a quiet corner for two minutes before you get dressed for your sport. Sit in silence and invite God's peace in.

25

SCARED OF BEING GREAT

"For the Spirit God gave us does not make us timid, but gives us power, love and self-discipline." — 2 Timothy 1:7

Lisa Leslie changed women's basketball forever. She was the first woman to dunk in a WNBA game. But stepping into greatness is scary. Sometimes we shrink back because we don't want to look like a show-off or we are afraid of the responsibility. Lisa had to embrace the spirit of power, not timidity. She realized God didn't make her tall and talented to hide in the corner. He made her to lead. Maybe you hold back in practice. Maybe you pass the ball when you should take the shot because you don't want to stand out. Stop hiding. God gave you that talent on purpose. Being timid insults the Giver of the gift. Being disciplined and powerful honors Him. Don't apologize for being fast. Don't say sorry for being strong. Step into the spotlight, not for your ego, but to show what God can do. Be great. It is what you were made for. Play big because your God is big.

Prayer:

Lord, forgive me for shrinking back. I accept Your spirit of power. Help me lead and play big for Your glory. Amen.

Practice:

Do one thing today that requires leadership—encourage a teammate loudly or take the tough shot. refuse to hide.

26
TRUSTING MY GUT

"But when he, the Spirit of truth, comes, he will guide you into all the truth." — John 16:13

Tamika Catchings is a legend, but she grew up with a hearing impairment. On the court, she couldn't always hear the play calls or the whistle. She had to rely on something else—her instincts and her vision. She learned to trust her gut, which she tuned to God's Spirit. She became one of the best defenders in history because she anticipated plays before they happened. You have a helper too. The Holy Spirit isn't just for church; He guides you in truth everywhere. Sometimes on the field, you have a split second to decide. Pass or shoot? Swing or take? Trust that inner prompt. When you walk closely with God, He sharpens your instincts. You stop hesitating. You start flowing. Don't ignore that quiet nudge in your gut. It is often God guiding you to the right spot at the right time. Trust your preparation, and trust the Spirit within you. He speaks in feelings and nudges, so listen closely.

Prayer:

Holy Spirit, sharpen my instincts. Guide my decisions on and off the field. I trust Your nudges and direction. Amen.

Practice:

Play a practice game where you make decisions instantly without second-guessing. Trust your first instinct and see what happens.

27
INTIMIDATED BY THEM

"The Lord is my light and my salvation—whom shall I fear?" — Psalm 27:1

Jocelyn Alo, the home run queen of softball, faced pitchers who wanted to strike her out every single time. They stared her down. They threw fast. It is easy to look at the opponent and feel small. Their jerseys look nicer, they look taller, their warm-up looks professional. Intimidation is a liar. It tricks you into thinking they are giants and you are a grasshopper. Jocelyn stepped into the box knowing who her Light was. When God is your salvation, a pitcher is just a person. A goalie is just a girl. They put their socks on one foot at a time, just like you. Do not give them power over your mind. Respect their skill, yes, but do not fear them. You have the Lord of Armies on your side. Stand tall in the batter's box. Look them in the eye. You are a daughter of the King. Whom shall you fear? Absolutely no one. Play with the confidence of a champion who knows who wins in the end.

Prayer:

God, You are my light. I refuse to be intimidated by any opponent. Remind me that You are bigger than any giant I face. Amen.

Practice:

Look your opponent in the eye during the coin toss or handshake. Smile confidently. Remind yourself: "God is with me."

28
REPLAYING MY SCREW-UPS

"Because of the Lord's great love we are not consumed, for his compassions never fail. They are new every morning." — Lamentations 3:22-23

Anna Hall competes in the heptathlon. That is seven different events. If she messes up the high jump, she has to run hurdles. If she is slow in the hurdles, she has to throw the shot put. There is no time to sulk. Anna knows that if she replays her screw-ups, she will lose the whole meet. She needs new mercies for every single event. You might have had a terrible first half. Maybe you fumbled or missed a block. The enemy wants you to watch a replay of that mistake in your head all game long. Don't let him. God's compassion is new right now. Not just every morning, but every timeout, every whistle, every quarter. You are not consumed by your failure. You are loved by God. Take a breath. Accept the new mercy. Step into the next event with a clean slate. Your past performance does not define your next play. God is ready to help you now, regardless of what happened five minutes ago.

Prayer:

Lord, thank You for new chances. I let go of my mistakes from the past. I step into this new moment with fresh focus. Amen.

Practice:

If you mess up, untie and retie your shoe. Let that action symbolize a fresh start and a new mercy.

29

JUST BREATHE, GIRL

"Then the Lord God formed a man from the dust of the ground and breathed into his nostrils the breath of life." — Genesis 2:7

Simone Manuel made history in the pool, but swimming is all about rhythm. If you fight the water, you sink. If you hold your breath out of panic, you gas out. Simone finds a rhythm in her stroke that is almost like worship. Breathing is the first gift God gave us. In the middle of a high-pressure game, we often forget to do it. We clench our jaw. We hold our breath. Our muscles get tight and our brain gets foggy. You need to return to the breath of life. When the game speeds up, slow your breathing down. Inhale through your nose, exhale through your mouth. It tells your brain, "I am safe. I am in control." It connects you back to the Creator who gave you that breath. Don't panic. Just breathe. Find your rhythm. God is sustaining you with every single lungful of air. You are alive, you are capable, and you are His. Breathe in His peace.

Prayer:

Creator God, thank You for the breath in my lungs. When I panic, help me slow down, breathe deep, and find Your rhythm. Amen.

Practice:

Practice "box breathing" on the bench: Inhale 4 seconds, hold 4 seconds, exhale 4 seconds, hold 4 seconds. Repeat.

CHAPTER 3: DAILY FAITHFULNESS WINS

30
I RUN UNTIL I PUKE

"No, I strike a blow to my body and make it my slave so that after I have preached to others, I myself will not be disqualified for the prize." (1 Corinthians 9:27)

The stadium is empty and the lights are buzzing. Sydney McLaughlin-Levrone is not smiling for a camera. She is bent over on the track with her hands on her knees. Her lungs burn like fire. Her legs feel like heavy jelly. This is not the glamorous moment of standing on the Olympic podium with a gold medal around her neck. This is the dark place where the gold is actually earned. Sydney views track as a ministry, but she knows her body naturally wants to quit. It wants comfort. It wants to stop. So she trains harder than anyone else to tell her body who is in charge. She runs until she feels sick so that when the race comes, her body knows how to obey.

You might hate sprints at the end of practice. You might despise holding a plank until you shake. It hurts. But that pain is not there to break you. It is there to build you. You are teaching your body that your spirit is the boss. When you push through the "I can't," you are building a discipline that lasts forever.

Prayer:

God, give me the strength to push past comfort. Help me discipline my body to honor You. Amen.

Practice:

Do one extra sprint or rep today when you are tired. Tell your body "I am in charge."

31

I HATE THIS DRILL

"No discipline seems pleasant at the time, but painful. Later on, however, it produces a harvest of righteousness and peace for those who have been trained by it." (Hebrews 12:11)

Sheryl Swoopes is a basketball legend, the first player signed to the WNBA. She had three MVP trophies and four championships. She could have coasted on her talent. Yet, even late in her career, observers would find her in an empty gym doing the most boring drills imaginable. Defensive slides. Basic ball handling. The squeak of her sneakers echoed in the quiet gym. She did the things rookies do because she knew fundamentals crumble under pressure if you ignore them. She did not love the drill itself. She loved the "harvest" the drill produced in the fourth quarter.

You probably have a drill you dread. Maybe it is lane slides or burpees. It feels repetitive and useless. It is boring. But boredom is where champions are made. The flashy plays you see on Instagram are built on hours of boring repetition in the dark. Change your mind about the work you hate. Don't look at the drill. Look at the reward waiting on the other side of it.

Prayer:

Lord, help me trust the process. When I am bored or tired, remind me of the harvest coming. Amen.

Practice:

Pick the drill you hate the most. Do it with 100% effort today without complaining once.

32
FUELING MY TEMPLE

"Do you not know that your bodies are temples of the Holy Spirit, who is in you, whom you have received from God? You are not your own." (1 Corinthians 6:19)

Michelle Akers was the warrior of 90s soccer. She played hard and hit harder. But then her body shut down. She was diagnosed with Chronic Fatigue Syndrome. She would collapse on the field, totally drained. To keep playing the sport she loved, she had to change everything. She could not eat junk. She could not skip hydration. She realized her body was not just a tool for sports, but a temple given by God. She treated her nutrition like medicine. Because she fueled her temple with precision, she extended her career and won the World Cup. It is easy to grab fast food after a game or skip breakfast before school. You feel fine now, so you think it does not matter. But your body is a high-performance engine. You cannot put sludge in a race car and expect it to win. What you eat and drink today decides how you run tomorrow. Respect the body God gave you by giving it the premium fuel it needs to perform.

Prayer:

Father, thank You for my body. Help me treat it with respect and fuel it for Your glory. Amen.

Practice:

Drink one extra bottle of water today and replace one sugary snack with fruit or protein.

33
SLEEP IS MY WEAPON

"In vain you rise early and stay up late, toiling for food to eat—for he grants sleep to those he loves." (Psalm 127:2)

Snowboarding is dangerous. You are flying twenty feet in the air above an icy halfpipe. One split-second mistake means a crash. Kelly Clark dominated this sport for twenty years. That is almost impossible in snowboarding. Her secret weapon was not a new board. It was sleep. While other competitors stayed up late partying or hanging out, Kelly went to bed. She prioritized rest like it was a training session. She knew that her brain needed to repair itself to keep her reaction times fast and her body strong. She viewed sleep as the ultimate trust in God. You live in a world that never stops. Your phone pings all night. You have homework and shows to watch. But cutting sleep cuts your performance. Your muscles repair when you dream. Your focus sharpens when you rest. Going to bed early is a discipline. It takes guts to turn the lights out when everyone else is online. Make sleep your secret weapon for success.

Prayer:

God, help me trust You enough to rest. Quiet my mind so I can sleep and recover. Amen.

Practice:

Set a "tech curfew" tonight. Phone off and away from your bed 30 minutes before you sleep.

34
I DON'T WANT TO

"Father, if you are willing, take this cup from me; yet not my will, but yours be done." (Luke 22:42)

Maya Moore is one of the greatest winners in basketball history. But she shocked the world when she walked away from the WNBA at the peak of her powers. She felt called to fight for justice reform. It was hard. She missed the game. She missed the paycheck. But she knew obedience matters more than feelings. Even in practice, Maya was known for doing the things she did not want to do. Boxing out. Running the floor. She understood that "I don't want to" is a feeling, not a fact. Jesus felt the weight of the cross and asked for another way, yet He still obeyed.

There will be mornings you do not want to wake up. There will be practices you do not want to attend. Your feelings will scream "no." Listen to the Holy Spirit instead. Doing the right thing when you don't feel like it is the definition of character. Do not let your mood dictate your motion.

Prayer:

Lord, help me obey even when I don't want to. Let Your will be stronger than my feelings. Amen.

Practice:

Identify one task you have been avoiding. Do it immediately. Do not think, just do.

35
SHOWING UP EARLY MATTERS

"Let us not become weary in doing good, for at the proper time we will reap a harvest if we do not give up." (Galatians 6:9)

The stadium is quiet. The fans have not arrived. But Julie Ertz is already there. Before she became a two-time World Cup champion, she was known for a blue-collar work ethic. She did not just show up to play; she showed up to prepare. While others were rushing from the locker room tying their shoes, Julie was already sweating. She was stretching, visualizing, and preparing her mind. She treated the warmup as importantly as the kickoff. That preparation allowed her to play faster and harder than everyone else when the whistle finally blew. If you arrive at practice right when it starts, you are actually late. Your body might be there, but your mind is still catching up. Rushing creates stress. Arriving early creates peace. It gives you time to pray, to stretch, and to switch your brain into "athlete mode." It shows your coach you respect their time. It shows God you value the opportunity to play.

Prayer:

Father, help me value preparation. Let me honor my team and You by showing up ready to work. Amen.

Practice:

Arrive 15 minutes early to your next practice or meeting. Use that time to stretch and pray.

36
RESPECTING MY GEAR

"Whoever can be trusted with very little can also be trusted with much..." (Luke 16:10)

Hockey equipment smells bad and costs a lot. It is heavy and bulky. It is easy to throw it in the corner after a long game. But Gigi Marvin, an Olympic gold medalist, treats her gear differently. She knows that every skate, stick, and pad is a gift. She takes care of her equipment because she is grateful she gets to play. She understands that if you cannot take care of your physical tools, you cannot be trusted with bigger opportunities. How you treat your things shows the condition of your heart.

Do you throw your helmet when you are mad? Do you leave your cleats caked in mud? Do you lose your uniform? This is not just about being messy. It is about stewardship. God provided that gear, likely through the hard work of your parents. When you take care of your stuff, you are saying "thank you." Respect your tools, and they will take care of you in the game.

Prayer:

God, thank You for the gear I have. Help me to be a good steward of every gift. Amen.

Practice:

Clean your gear today. Wipe down your shoes, organize your bag, and put everything in its place.

37
HURT VS INJURED

"Not only so, but we also glory in our sufferings, because we know that suffering produces perseverance; perseverance, character..." (Romans 5:3-4)

Anna Hall was a favorite to win a medal in the heptathlon. Then, disaster struck. She broke a bone in her foot. The pain was sharp and real. She had a choice to make. Athletes live on a fine line. There is being "hurt," which is soreness and bruising. Then there is being "injured," where playing causes damage. Anna had to use wisdom. She healed, rehabbed, and came back to win silver at the World Championships, pushing through incredible discomfort. She learned that some pain is a stop sign, but some pain is just the price of greatness.

You need to know your body. Being an athlete means you will be sore. You will have bruises. You will be tired. That is "hurt," and you push through that. That builds perseverance. But sharp pain is a warning light. Do not ignore it to look tough. God gave you wisdom. Learn the difference so you can have a long career, not just a good season.

Prayer:

Lord, give me wisdom to know my body. Help me push through discomfort but protect me from injury. Amen.

Practice:

Do a body scan. Is it soreness or injury? If sore, stretch. If injured, tell your coach.

38
GETTING 1% BETTER TODAY

"A sluggard's appetite is never filled, but the desires of the diligent are fully satisfied." (Proverbs 13:4)

The ocean is unpredictable. No two waves are the same. Carissa Moore, a five-time world champion surfer, cannot control the water. She can only control herself. She does not try to become a legend in one day. She focuses on getting 1% better. Maybe it is just her pop-up. Maybe it is just her balance on one turn. She knows that small, diligent improvements stack up over time. If you improve 1% every day, by the end of the year, you are a completely different athlete.

You often want to be perfect right now. You miss a shot and think you are a failure. Stop looking at the whole mountain. Just look at the next step. What is one tiny thing you can fix today? Maybe it is your footwork. Maybe it is your attitude. Don't try to fix everything at once. Be diligent in the small things. The big results will take care of themselves.

Prayer:

God, save me from the pressure of perfection. Help me focus on getting a little better today. Amen.

Practice:

Pick one specific, small skill to improve today. Focus only on that during practice.

39
GRADES KEEP ME PLAYING

"And whatever you do, whether in word or deed, do it all in the name of the Lord Jesus..." (Colossians 3:17)

The world knows Caitlin Clark for her deep three-pointers and record-breaking scoring. But before she was a household name, she was a student. She was an Academic All-American. She did not ignore the classroom to focus on the court. She understood that how you do anything is how you do everything. You cannot be lazy in math class and then expect to be disciplined in the fourth quarter. Excellence is a habit, not a switch you flip on for sports. Caitlin kept her grades up because she wanted to honor God with her mind, not just her jump shot. It is tempting to blow off homework because you are tired from practice. But your grades are your ticket to play. More importantly, your work ethic in school builds the mental toughness you need for sports. Don't be a player who needs a tutor to stay eligible. Be a champion who dominates the history test just like the game.

Prayer:

Lord, help me honor You in the classroom. Give me focus to finish my work with excellence. Amen.

Practice:

Finish your homework before you touch your phone or video games tonight. Do it with excellence.

40

PUT THE PHONE DOWN

"Be very careful, then, how you live—not as unwise but as wise, making the most of every opportunity..." (Ephesians 5:15-16)

Beach volleyball player Kelly Cheng travels the world. She spends hours in airports and hotels. It is so easy to pull out a phone and doom-scroll through social media for hours. You see what everyone else is doing. You compare your life to theirs. It drains your mental battery. Kelly decided to make a change. Instead of scrolling, she started opening her Bible or a book. She chose to fill her mind with truth instead of noise. This kept her focused and peaceful, while her opponents were distracted and anxious.

Your phone is a tool, but it can also be a trap. Comparing yourself to other athletes on Instagram steals your joy. Scrolling late at night steals your sleep. You have limited time every day. Be wise with it. Imagine how much stronger your mind would be if you replaced 20 minutes of TikTok with 20 minutes of reading or prayer. Protect your focus.

Prayer:

Father, help me guard my time. Give me the strength to put the phone down and focus on You. Amen.

Practice:

Turn off all notifications for one hour today. Use that time to read, pray, or go outside.

41
WHY CAN'T I TALK BACK?

"Slaves, obey your earthly masters with respect and fear, and with sincerity of heart, just as you would obey Christ." (Ephesians 6:5)

Dominique Moceanu was part of the "Magnificent Seven" gymnastics team. She won Olympic gold at age 14. She had incredibly tough coaches. They were demanding and sometimes harsh. It would have been easy to roll her eyes, talk back, or storm off. But gymnastics requires safety and precision. If you are not listening, you get hurt. She learned to respect the position of the coach, even when it was hard. She kept her dignity, but she followed instructions. This discipline allowed her to reach the top of the podium   You might have a coach who yells. You might have a teacher who is unfair. You want to talk back. You want to argue. But talking back shows a lack of self-control. Respecting authority does not mean you are weak; it means you are disciplined. You can respectfully ask questions, but rolling your eyes helps nothing. Listen to instruction. It is a sign of maturity that sets you apart.

Prayer:

God, help me to respect those in authority over me. Give me a humble heart and a teachable spirit. Amen.

Practice:

The next time a coach or parent corrects you, look them in the eye and simply say, "Okay."

42

LEADING WITHOUT SPEAKING

"Don't let anyone look down on you because you are young, but set an example for the believers in speech, in conduct, in love, in faith and in purity." (1 Timothy 4:12)

Aliyah Boston is a force in women's basketball. She dominates the paint. But you rarely see her screaming at her teammates or demanding the ball. She leads by doing. She boxes out every single time. She runs the floor hard even when she doesn't get the pass. Her teammates watch her effort and they step up their game. They trust her because she works harder than anyone else. She sets an example with her sweat, not her mouth. Her conduct makes her a captain, not just her title.   You might think leading means giving a big speech in the huddle. But if you talk big and play lazy, no one will listen. True leadership is visual. Be the first one in line for drills. Pick up the trash on the bench. High-five the teammate who made a mistake. Lead with your actions. Your team will follow your feet long before they follow your voice.

Prayer:

Lord, let my actions speak louder than my words. Help me lead my team by serving and working hard. Amen.

Practice:

Encourage three teammates today and be the first person to start cleaning up after practice.

43

IT'S OKAY TO REST

"Come with me by yourselves to a quiet place and get some rest." (Mark 6:31)

Simone Biles is the greatest gymnast of all time. The world expected her to win everything in Tokyo. But then, she got the "twisties." Her mind and body disconnected. It was dangerous. She did something shocking: she withdrew. She stepped back. The world had opinions, but Simone knew the truth. She was not quitting; she was healing. She realized that her worth was not in her medals. She needed to rest her mind to save her soul. By taking a break, she showed the world that mental health matters more than trophies.

Sometimes you feel like you have to keep going until you crash. You think rest is for the weak. That is a lie. Even Jesus pulled away from the crowds to rest and pray. If your brain is tired, your performance suffers. If your heart is heavy, your game breaks down. Taking a step back to breathe is not quitting. It is how you recharge so you can return stronger.

Prayer:

Father, thank You that I don't have to earn Your love. Help me to rest without guilt when I need it. Amen.

Practice:

Take 10 minutes today to sit in total silence. No music, no phone. Just breathe and be with God.

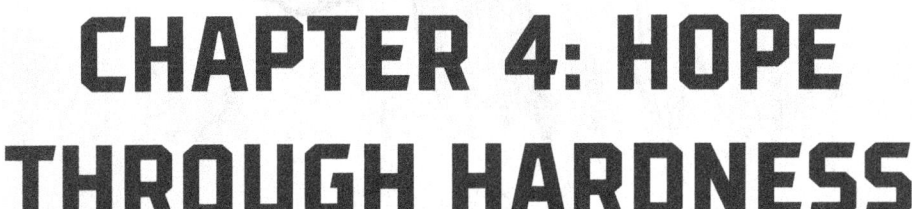

CHAPTER 4: HOPE THROUGH HARDNESS

44

GOD, WHERE ARE YOU?

"How long, Lord? Will you forget me forever? How long will you hide your face from me?" (Psalm 13:1)

The water was crystal clear and the sun felt perfect. Bethany Hamilton floated on her surfboard, surrounded by friends, feeling peace. Then, the water turned red. In a violent second, a shark took her arm and shattered her world. Rushed to the hospital, losing blood, the question screamed louder than the pain: "God, why? Why me? Why now?"   It is easy to trust God when standing on a podium holding a trophy. It is harder when staring at a hospital ceiling, wondering if life is over. Bethany had to decide if her faith was based on circumstances or her Creator. She realized God did not leave the water when the shark came; He was holding her through the rescue. You might feel abandoned due to injury or loss. Pain begs us to believe God is absent, but Scripture says He is close to the brokenhearted. Silence does not mean He is gone. He is preparing you for a comeback that will shout His glory louder than your win ever could.

Prayer:

Lord, even when I hurt and cannot see You, help me trust that You are holding me close. Amen.

Practice:

Write down one hard thing happening right now. Next to it write: "God is still with me here."

45

WHY DID I GET HURT?

"Neither this man nor his parents sinned," said Jesus, "but this happened so that the works of God might be displayed in him." (John 9:3)

Paige Bueckers moves across the basketball court like water. She is fast, sharp, and unstoppable. But when her knee buckled and the diagnosis came back as a torn ACL, the arena went silent. The sneakers and cheers stopped. For an athlete, the body is your tool; when it breaks, it feels like punishment. Paige had to sit while her team played on, watching from the sideline with crutches in hand.   It would have been easy to stay bitter or jealous. Instead, she realized this pause was not a penalty; it was a stage. Jesus taught that some trials happen so God can show His power in our recovery. Your injury is not a stop sign. It is a detour toward a different strength. When you sit out, you learn to see the game differently. You learn that your worth is not in your vertical leap but in who God says you are. Be still and trust God's work within you. Trust the healing process.

Prayer:

Jesus, help me see this injury not as a punishment, but as a place for Your power to shine. Amen.

Practice:

While you heal, find one way to serve your team from the sidelines. cheering, water, or just encouragement.

46

LOSING WITHOUT LOSING MYSELF

"Though the fig tree does not bud... yet I will rejoice in the Lord, I will be joyful in God my Savior." (Habakkuk 3:17-18)

The track at the Beijing Olympics was a blur of red and white. Lolo Jones was flying. She was leading the 100 meter hurdles, the Gold Medal waiting at the finish line. Then, her foot clipped the ninth hurdle. She stumbled. The rhythm broke. She watched competitors zoom past as she faded to seventh place. The world watched her collapse in tears. It was the moment every athlete fears. Yet, Lolo knew her soul was anchored to something heavier than gold. Habakkuk speaks of rejoicing even when the crops fail and the barns are empty. For you, that means praising God when the scoreboard says you lost. It means knowing you are a champion before the race even starts because you belong to Him. One bad race, missed shot, or stumble does not change your value. You can handle heartbreak because your joy comes from the Savior who never loses. If identity is built on winning, you crumble. Built on Jesus, you are unbreakable.

Prayer:

God, be my joy when I win and my strength when I lose. My identity is safe in You. Amen.

Practice:

After your next practice or game, say "Thank you God for the ability to play," regardless of the result.

47

THE COMEBACK IS COMING

"See, I am doing a new thing! Now it springs up; do you not perceive it? I will make a way in the wilderness." (Isaiah 43:19)

Gabby Douglas stood on the balance beam, gravity trying to pull her down. Before she became the first African American all around Olympic gold medalist, she was just a teenager who wanted to quit. Bad practices piled up. She felt homesick and tired. The skills were not clicking. She told her mom she was done. But God was preparing a "new thing" in the gym. He was refining her form and her heart in the quiet, frustrating days. Isaiah promises that God makes roads in the wilderness and rivers in the desert. You might feel stuck in a slump right now. Maybe your times are getting slower or your form feels off. Do not mistake a rough season for a dead end. God is often doing His best work when we feel like we are making zero progress. Shake off the bad practice. The breakthrough is springing up. Keep showing up, because the comeback is already being written. Your struggle is just the setup for the new thing God is about to do in your life.

Prayer:

Lord, I trust You are doing a new thing in me. Give me the grit to keep going. Amen.

Practice:

When you make a mistake today, say "Reset" out loud and focus immediately on the very next play.

48

THAT CALL WAS UNFAIR!

"Commit your way to the Lord; trust in him and he will do this: He will make your righteous reward shine like the dawn." (Psalm 37:5-6)

The Rio Olympic track shone under the stadium lights. Allyson Felix sprinted the 400 meters, lungs burning, legs pumping. She was inches from Gold. Then, the runner next to her dove. Literally threw herself across the line. Allyson stayed on her feet, crossing upright, but the dive won by 0.07 seconds. It felt cheap. It felt wrong. Millions argued about it online. But Allyson did not throw a fit. She congratulated the winner. She smiled through the disappointment. She knew Psalm 37. You can scream at the ref, throw your helmet, and blame the umpire, or you can commit your way to the Lord. Unfair calls are going to happen. Coaches will have favorites. Refs will miss fouls. If you let that anger consume you, you lose your focus. Trust that God sees the truth. Your character shines brighter than a medal when you handle unfairness with grace. Let God handle the justice. You handle the running. Winners do not waste energy on things they cannot control. They trust God and keep moving forward.

Prayer:

Father, help me stay cool when things are unfair. I trust You to defend me so I can focus. Amen.

Practice:

The next time a call goes against you, take a deep breath and refuse to complain. Play harder instead.

49
MY COACH IS TOXIC

"If it is possible, as far as it depends on you, live at peace with everyone." (Romans 12:18)

Mary Pierce played tennis with power, but her hardest battles were not against opponents. They were against the man in her box. Her father was her coach, and he was abusive. He yelled, he embarrassed her, and he made the game a prison of fear. It is hard to swing freely when you are terrified of making a mistake. Mary eventually had to set boundaries for her safety, but she also found Jesus. She learned that while she could not control her father, she could control her reaction. Romans tells us to live at peace as far as it depends on us. You might have a coach who yells too much or puts you down. It hurts. You cannot fix them, but you can guard your heart. Play for God, not for the angry voice on the sideline. Respect the position, follow instructions, but do not let their toxicity become your inner voice. Your Heavenly Father coaches with love, not fear. Do not let a human break the spirit God gave you. Stay focused on your game.

Prayer:

Lord, give me peace when people are difficult. Protect my heart from harsh words and help me listen to You. Amen.

Practice:

Identify one thing you love about your sport. Focus on that joy today, blocking out any negative noise.

50

SUFFERING MAKES ME STRONGER

"Consider it pure joy, my brothers and sisters, whenever you face trials of many kinds, because you know that the testing of your faith produces perseverance." (James 1:2-4)

Kerri Walsh Jennings dominates the sand. She is a volleyball icon with three gold medals. But her shoulder was a constant battleground. Five surgeries. Five times of rebuilding muscle, relearning motion, and sitting in pain while others played. It would be easy to call it bad luck. Kerri calls it training. Just as lifting heavy weights tears muscle to build it back stronger, suffering tears at our spirit to build perseverance. James tells us to count it as joy. That sounds crazy until you see the result. The trials you face in sports—the conditioning drills that make you want to throw up, the injuries, the losses—are not just physical. They are spiritual reps. God is building a version of you that does not quit. When you are hurting, you are growing. Do not waste the pain. Let it do its work so you can stand on the court complete and lacking nothing. A smooth sea never made a skilled sailor, and an easy season never made a champion. Embrace the grind.

Prayer:

God, I choose to see this challenge as training. Build my perseverance and make me stronger through this trial. Amen.

Practice:

During the hardest part of your workout, whisper "This is making me stronger" instead of complaining about the pain.

51
I'VE GOT THE YIPS

"For the Spirit God gave us does not make us timid, but gives us power, love and self-discipline." (2 Timothy 1:7)

Simone Biles floated high above the gymnastics mat in Tokyo. She is the greatest of all time, but suddenly, she was lost in the air. The "twisties" had struck. Her brain and body disconnected. The danger was real. The pressure of the world sat on her shoulders, and fear crept in. She chose to step back to protect herself. It was a brave move. But she also knew fear was not her master. Scripture says God gives us a spirit of power and a sound mind. When you get the "yips"—when you suddenly cannot make the throw or land the jump—it is often fear disguised as failure. Pause. Breathe. Remember that your talent comes from a God of order, not chaos. You have the spirit of self discipline. You can step back, reset your mind, and step back in. Fear is a liar. The power inside you is real. Do not force it. Let God restore your confidence piece by piece. You are safe in His hands.

Prayer:

Jesus, calm my mind. Remove the spirit of fear and replace it with Your power and clear thinking. Amen.

Practice:

Visualize yourself doing your skill perfectly three times before you go to sleep. See it. Believe it.

52

WAITING FOR MY TURN

"Wait for the Lord; be strong and take heart and wait for the Lord." (Psalm 27:14)

Carly Lloyd is a soccer legend, but she started on the bench. She watched others get the glory. She watched the clock tick down. It burns to sit there. You feel invisible. You feel like the coach is making a mistake. Abby Wambach, another legend, also had to learn the role of a substitute later in her career. Both women found that the bench is not a trash can; it is a classroom. David waited years to be King. You are waiting for your minutes. Psalm 27 commands us to be strong while we wait. Do not pout. Study the game. Watch the opponent's defense. Cheer for your teammates. Prepare your mind so that when your number is finally called, you are not cold and bitter, but hot and ready. Your time is coming. God is working on your character while you wait for the whistle. Being a good teammate on the bench is harder than being a star on the field. Prove you can handle both.

Prayer:

Lord, help me wait with a good attitude. Keep me ready and humble. I trust Your timing for me. Amen.

Practice:

If you are on the bench, pick one player on the field and watch everything they do to learn.

53

WE GOT DESTROYED

"We are hard pressed on every side, but not crushed; perplexed, but not in despair." (2 Corinthians 4:8-9)

The scoreboard was ugly. The Tennessee Lady Vols didn't just lose; they got crushed. In the locker room, heads hung low. The silence was heavy. It feels embarrassing to walk off the court when you have been dominated. You want to hide. Pat Summitt, their legendary coach, would stare them down. She knew that a blowout loss tests your culture more than a win. Paul wrote to the Corinthians that we can be struck down but not destroyed. You lost a game, you did not lose your soul. A champion team takes the beating, watches the film, fixes the holes, and comes back the next day with fire. Do not let one humiliation define your season. Wipe the tears, tie your shoes, and get back in the gym. Being "hard pressed" is just how diamonds are made. You are not crushed. You are just under construction. The only real failure is refusing to get back up. Use the embarrassment as fuel to ensure it never happens again.

Prayer:

Father, I hurt from this loss, but I am not broken. Help me rise up, learn, and try again. Amen.

Practice:

Write down two specific things the other team did better than you. Practice those two things this week.

54
DON'T GET COCKY

"Pride goes before destruction, a haughty spirit before a fall." (Proverbs 16:18)

Lisa Leslie changed basketball. She was the first woman to dunk in a WNBA game. She dominated the paint, blocked shots, and scored at will. It would have been easy to think she was the only reason her team won. But Lisa knew that the moment you think you are untouchable, you are in danger. Proverbs warns us that pride is a setup for a crash. Confidence says, "I have worked hard and I can do this." Cockiness says, "I am better than everyone and I don't need to try." Cockiness makes you lazy. It makes you ignore your coach. It makes you disrespect your opponent. True strength is meekness—power under control. Stay hungry. The best athletes know there is always someone working in a gym somewhere to beat them. Give glory to God for your talent, and keep working like you are still fighting for your spot. A humble athlete is a dangerous athlete because they never stop learning. Keep your eyes on God, not your stats, and you will stay on track.

Prayer:

God, thank You for my talent. Keep me humble. Remind me that every good gift comes from You. Amen.

Practice:

After a great game, compliment a teammate on something they did well before you talk about your own stats.

55
I'M NOT GETTING BETTER

"Let us not become weary in doing good, for at the proper time we will reap a harvest if we do not give up." (Galatians 6:9)

Keni Harrison was one of the best hurdlers in the world. But at the U.S. Olympic Trials, she had a bad race. She missed the team. She would not go to Rio. The devastation was total. She had trained for years for a door that just slammed shut. It felt like all her work was wasted. But Keni went back to the track. She didn't quit. A few weeks later, she ran again. She didn't just win; she broke the World Record. Galatians promises a harvest if we do not give up. You might feel like you are plateauing. You are lifting, running, and training, but you aren't getting faster. You aren't scoring more. Do not stop. The roots are growing deep even if the fruit isn't showing yet. Your "proper time" is coming. Just like Keni, your biggest breakdown might be right before your biggest breakthrough. Keep planting seeds. God sees every rep and every drop of sweat. Trust His timing, not your feelings.

Prayer:

Lord, I am tired of trying without seeing results. Help me trust that the harvest is coming. I won't quit. Amen.

Practice:

Commit to your training routine for two weeks regardless of how you "feel." Trust the process.

56
HEARING MY PARENTS YELL

"The one who has knowledge uses words with restraint, and whoever has understanding is even-tempered." (Proverbs 17:27)

Coco Gauff is a tennis prodigy, playing on massive courts with thousands of screaming fans. But sometimes the clearest voice she hears is her dad. He coached her from the start. Sometimes parents get loud. Sometimes they yell instructions when you are trying to focus. It can be annoying and embarrassing. You want to yell back, "I know!" Coco learned to filter. She separates the volume from the value. Proverbs speaks of being even tempered. When your parents are loud, or your coach is screaming, do not let their emotion wreck your calm. Listen for the truth in what they are saying—"Move your feet!" or "Watch the ball!"—and ignore the tone. They yell because they care, even if they do it wrong. Keep your cool. A cool spirit beats a hot head every time. You play the game; let them make the noise. Showing respect and staying focused, even when you are annoyed, is a sign of true maturity. God wants you to honor them by playing with a peaceful heart.

Prayer:

Father, help me honor my parents even when they stress me out. Give me a calm spirit to focus. Amen.

Practice:

Talk to your parents calmly before the game. Ask them what kind of support helps you best.

57
I HATE SECOND PLACE

"Do you not know that in a race all the runners run, but only one gets the prize? Run in such a way as to get the prize." (1 Corinthians 9:24)

Lolo Jones knows the sting of silver. She knows the burn of fourth place—missing a medal by a heartbeat. The media says "you lost," but the athlete says "I'm close." It hurts to watch someone else stand on the top step while the anthem plays. You might feel jealous or angry. But Paul tells us in Corinthians to run for the prize. He doesn't say "run just to have fun." He says run to win. It is okay to hate losing. That drive is a gift from God. But do not let second place make you bitter; let it make you hungry. Let the gap between you and the winner become your fuel. God honors discipline. If you fell short today, it means there is more work to do tomorrow. Respect the winner, then go tie your shoes. The race isn't over. Run to win. God did not design you to be passive. He designed you to chase excellence with everything you have. Use that fire to train harder for the next race.

Prayer:

God, give me the drive to win and the grace to handle it when I don't. Help me work harder. Amen.

Practice:

If you lose a sprint or a drill, ask the person who beat you for one tip, then try to beat your own time.

58

STARTING OVER FROM SCRATCH

"Your beginnings will seem humble, so prosperous will your future be." (Job 8:7)

Bethany Hamilton stood on the beach with one arm. She had to relearn how to paddle. She had to relearn how to pop up. She wiped out over and over. She used to be a pro, and now she looked like a beginner. It is humbling to start over. Maybe you are recovering from surgery, switching positions, or learning a new sport entirely. You feel clumsy. You feel slow. You want to quit because you remember how good you used to be. Job reminds us that humble beginnings lead to prosperous futures. Do not despise the day of small things. Every wobble is a lesson. Every fall is data. God is not afraid of your weakness. He loves the process of building you up. Be patient with yourself. You are building a new foundation, and this one will be stronger than the last. The ocean is waiting. Get back in. Your future victory is not based on where you start, but on whether you have the courage to begin again.

Prayer:

Lord, I feel weak right now. Help me be patient as I learn. I trust that my future is bright. Amen.

Practice:

Celebrate one tiny improvement today. Did you balance longer? Did you run further? That is a win.

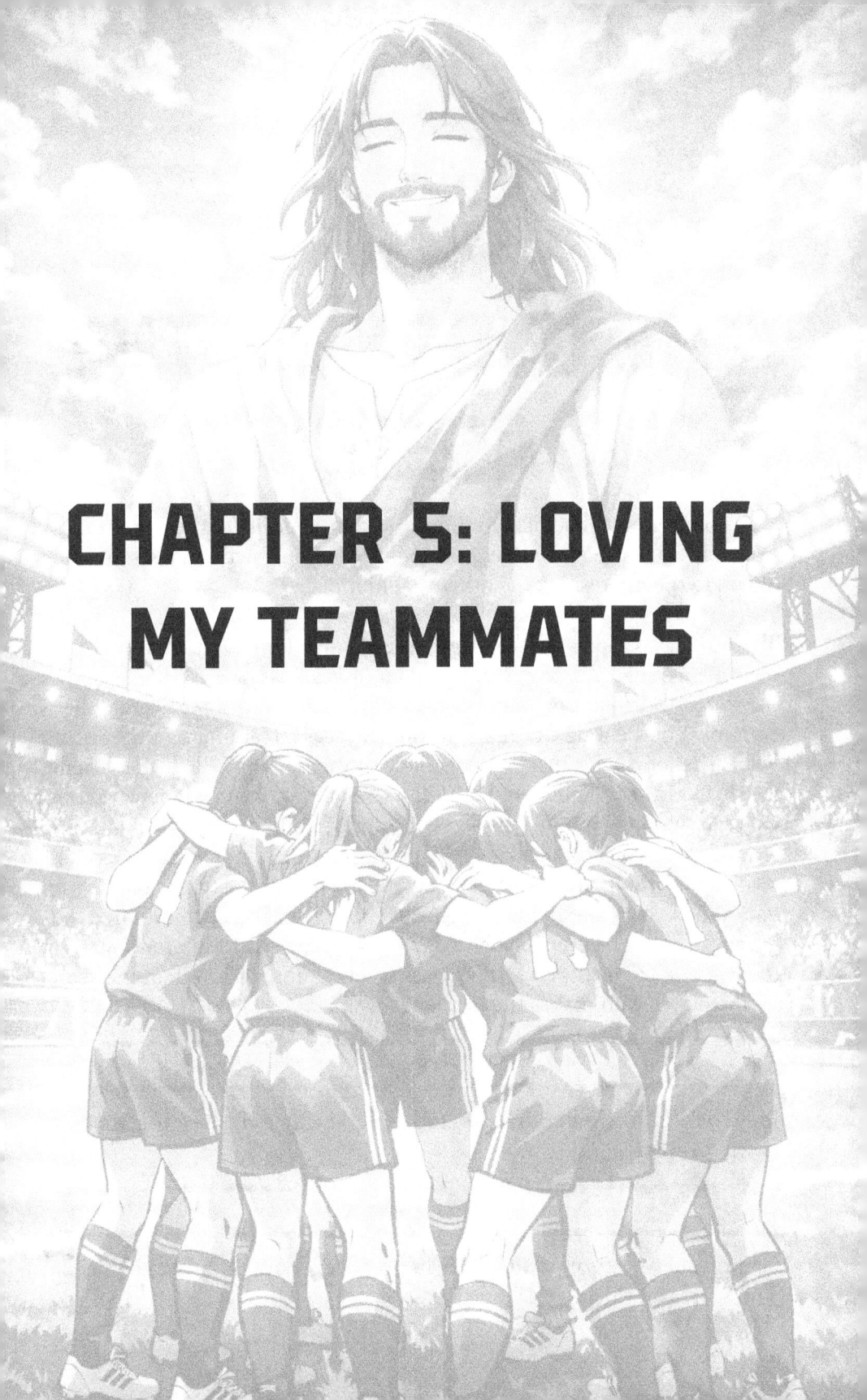

CHAPTER 5: LOVING MY TEAMMATES

59

THE GLORY OF THE ASSIST

"Do nothing out of selfish ambition or vain conceit. Rather, in humility value others above yourselves, not looking to your own interests but each of you to the interests of the others." (Philippians 2:3-4)

The buzzer sounds and the crowd erupts in a frenzy. But the highlight reel isn't a dunk or a deep three-pointer. It is a pass. Sue Bird, a legend in the WNBA, dribbles through heavy traffic. She could force a shot. She is certainly good enough to make it. But she sees a teammate in the corner with a better angle. In a split second, she whips the ball to her friend. Swish. Courtney Vandersloot does the same thing. These women are court generals who understand the secret power of Philippians 2. Real humility isn't thinking you are bad at sports. It is thinking of your teammate's success more than your own stats. When you hog the ball, the defense collapses on you. When you share it, the whole court opens up. You become dangerous because you make everyone else dangerous. Don't just look for your shot today. Look for the open girl. The assist takes more vision than the score. Be the player who makes the whole team shine.

Prayer:

Jesus, help me see my teammates today. Let me find joy in setting them up to win. Amen.

Practice:

Count your assists or good passes in practice today. High-five the person who scores off them.

60

SHUT DOWN THE GOSSIP

"A perverse person stirs up conflict, and a gossip separates close friends."
(Proverbs 16:28)

The locker room is quiet, but the whispers are loud. It is easy to bond over complaining. You talk about the coach's confusing drills or how the striker missed an easy goal. It feels like you are making friends, but you are actually planting poison. Tobin Heath, a creative force for the USWNT, is a Jesus follower first. In high-pressure tournaments, stress is high. One whisper can break the trust of a squad. Proverbs 16 warns that gossip separates friends. It acts like a wedge. Tobin chooses to be a fountain of life rather than a drain. When you hear teammates tearing someone down, you have a choice. You can join in, or you can change the subject. Real leaders protect their teammates' reputations even when they are not in the room. If you want a winning culture, you have to kill the gossip. Be the safe place where people are lifted up, not cut down. A united team is an unstoppable team.

Prayer:

Lord, guard my mouth. Let no unwholesome talk come out of me. Make me a peacemaker. Amen.

Practice:

If someone starts gossiping today, say something nice about that person or change the subject immediately.

61

GIVING MAKES YOU WIN

"In everything I did, I showed you that by this kind of hard work we must help the weak, remembering the words the Lord Jesus himself said: 'It is more blessed to give than to receive.'" (Acts 20:35)

The arena is shaking. Everyone is watching Caitlin Clark. She is famous for her logo-range three-pointers. But watch her eyes. She drives to the hoop, drawing three defenders. Suddenly, she wraps a pass around her back to a teammate under the basket. Layup. The crowd goes wild. Caitlin knows that while scoring is fun, assisting is leadership. Acts 20:35 reminds us that giving is a blessing. In sports, giving the ball up often leads to the best result. It requires trust. It tells your teammate that you believe in them. When you play with a generous spirit, the ball finds energy. The offense flows. If you hold onto the ball too long, the play dies. If you move it, the defense gets dizzy. Be the engine of generosity. When you give your teammate a chance to score, you aren't losing the spotlight. You are winning the game. Giving makes you the most valuable player on the floor.

Prayer:

God, thank You for my team. Teach me the joy of giving and sharing the victory. Amen.

Practice:

Focus on "hockey assists" today. Make the pass that leads to the pass that scores.

62
FORGIVE THE BIG MISTAKE

"Bear with each other and forgive one another if any of you has a grievance against someone. Forgive as the Lord forgave you." (Colossians 3:13)

The striker slips. The ball rolls past her foot. The other team steals it and scores. The game is tied. It feels like the air was sucked out of the stadium. It is easy to roll your eyes or throw your hands up. But look at the defense of the USWNT. When a defender gets beat, her teammate slides over to cover. No glaring. No yelling. Just cover. Colossians 3 commands us to forgive as the Lord forgave us. In sports, a grudge is heavy. If you are mad at your goalie for missing a save, you play slower. You hesitate. You stop trusting. Great athletes have short memories regarding mistakes. They forgive instantly so they can get back to work. Your teammate knows she messed up. She doesn't need a lecture. She needs to know you still have her back. Forgive the error, reset the focus, and go win the next play together. That is how champions handle failure.

Prayer:

Father, help me let go of frustration. Help me forgive my teammates and myself quickly. Amen.

Practice:

If a teammate messes up today, be the first to tap them on the back and say "Next play."

63
FRIENDS OVER RIVALS

"For where you have envy and selfish ambition, there you find disorder and every evil practice." (James 3:16)

The lights of the Beijing Olympics were blinding. Shawn Johnson and Nastia Liukin were roommates. They were best friends. They were also fighting for the same Gold Medal. The media wanted a catfight. They wanted drama. But Shawn and Nastia knew James 3:16. Envy brings disorder. It rots the team from the inside. Instead of looking at each other with jealousy, they chose to be sisters. When Nastia won Gold, Shawn smiled and hugged her. When Shawn won Gold on the beam, Nastia cheered. They realized that another girl's success does not steal your talent. The podium is big enough for kindness. You will have teammates who play your position. You will have friends who get the start when you sit. Do not let jealousy win. Cheer for them. Push them to be better. When you celebrate their win, you defeat the enemy of envy and keep your heart pure. Your time to shine will come.

Prayer:

Jesus, take away my jealousy. Let me celebrate my friends with a true heart. I am enough. Amen.

Practice:

Identify the teammate you are most jealous of. Genuinely cheer for them at least once today.

64
PRAYER FOR THE BULLY

"But I tell you, love your enemies and pray for those who persecute you." (Matthew 5:44)

The bobsled track is ice cold and dangerous. But for Elana Meyers Taylor, the track wasn't the only hard part. She faced people who made fun of her race and her gender. They called her names. They didn't want her there. It hurts to be treated unfairly. You want to fight back. You want to scream. Jesus gives a harder instruction in Matthew 5. Love your enemies. Pray for them. Elana didn't let their hate slow her sled. She used her energy to focus and pray. She won medals while they stayed bitter. When an opponent trash talks you or a crowd boos you, do not get ugly. Do not lower yourself to their level. Pray for them. It sounds crazy, but it frees you. Their words bounce off because you know who you are in Christ. Let your victory on the scoreboard be your only response. You are called to be a champion of grace, even on the ice.

Prayer:

Lord, it is hard to love mean people. Give me strength to pray for them and focus. Amen.

Practice:

Write down the name of a rival or bully. Pray for God to bless them, then release it.

65

FIX IT FACE TO FACE

"If your brother or sister sins, go and point out their fault, just between the two of you. If they listen, you have won them over." (Matthew 18:15)

Sand is everywhere. The sun is hot. It is just Kerri Walsh and April Ross on the volleyball court. There are no subs. If they are mad at each other, they lose. Sometimes wires get crossed. A set is too low. A serve is missed. Frustration rises. Matthew 18 gives the game plan for conflict. Go directly to the person. Don't text your other friend about how annoying your teammate is. Don't complain to your mom in the car yet. Go to your teammate. Look them in the eye. Say, "Hey, we are off. Let's fix this." Kerri and April had to keep their partnership clear to win medals. Hidden anger is like an anchor. It drags the team down. Be brave enough to have the hard conversation. Keep the circle tight. When you resolve conflict face-to-face, you build a bond that pressure cannot break. Real strength is admitting there is a problem and working together to fix it.

Prayer:

God, give me courage to speak truth with love. Help me resolve conflicts quickly and directly. Amen.

Practice:

Is there a teammate you are avoiding? Go talk to them today. Clear the air.

66
MAKE ROOM AT THE TABLE

"Accept one another, then, just as Christ accepted you, in order to bring praise to God." (Romans 15:7)

Travel ball days are long. You are on a bus, then a plane, then a hotel. Janie Reed, an outfielder for Team USA softball, knows that chemistry isn't just built on the diamond. It is built at dinner. It is easy to sit with your best friends every time. It is comfortable. But look around. Is there a teammate eating alone? Is someone wearing headphones in the corner? Romans 15 tells us to accept one another. Exclusion hurts. It makes a player feel small, and small players don't make big plays. Janie made it a ministry to include people. Be the one who scoots over. Be the one who says, "Hey, come sit here." When everyone feels like they belong to the family, they will fight harder for the family during the game. Inclusion wins championships. Be the teammate who ensures no one is left on the outside looking in. Your kindness builds the team's power.

Prayer:

Jesus, open my eyes to the lonely. Help me be a welcomer on my team today. Amen.

Practice:

Sit with a different teammate at lunch or during a break. Ask them a question about themselves.

67

CHEER LOUD WHEN INJURED

"Remember your leaders, who spoke the word of God to you. Consider the outcome of their way of life and imitate their faith." (Hebrews 13:7)

Kelley O'Hara is a warrior. She plays hard. But even warriors get hurt. During the World Cup, she wasn't always on the field. Being benched with an injury is the hardest mental test. You feel useless. You feel invisible. But Kelley didn't pout. She stood on the sideline and became the loudest leader on the team. She filled water bottles. She yelled instructions. She hyped up the younger players. Hebrews 13 says to imitate good leaders. Kelley showed that you don't need cleats to lead. You need a voice and a heart. If you are injured or sitting on the bench, do not check out. Your energy feeds the players on the field. Be the spark. If you can't run, cheer. If you can't score, serve. Your attitude on the bench can be the reason the team wins the game. You are still a vital part of the mission, no matter where you stand.

Prayer:

Lord, I want to play, but if I must sit, let me lead. Use my voice. Amen.

Practice:

If you are on the bench, be the loudest encourager. Pick one player to hype up specifically.

68
YOUR VOICE IS ENERGY

"Therefore encourage one another and build each other up, just as in fact you are doing." (1 Thessalonians 5:11)

Gymnastics is usually silent. Judges are watching. Nerves are tight. But at the Rio Olympics, you could hear Laurie Hernandez. She was the youngest, but she was the spark plug. Before her teammates went to the beam or floor, Laurie was screaming, "You got this!" She smiled. She danced. She became known as the "Human Emoji." 1 Thessalonians 5:11 commands us to build each other up. Fear is contagious, but so is confidence. When the gym is quiet, doubt creeps in. Laurie's voice chased the doubt away. She reminded her team that they were ready. You have that same power. When your teammate is at the free-throw line or about to serve, they need to know you believe in them. Don't be too cool to cheer. Be the battery that charges the whole team. Your belief can make them brave. Speak life into your teammates and watch their performance rise to meet your words.

Prayer:

Father, let my words be fuel for my team. Help me speak courage into their hearts. Amen.

Practice:

Give three specific compliments to teammates during practice. "Great shot" or "Good hustle."

69
OWN YOUR MESS UP

"Therefore confess your sins to each other and pray for each other so that you may be healed." (James 5:16)

Julie Ertz was a beast in the midfield. She tackled hard and headed the ball with power. But soccer is a game of mistakes. Sometimes a pass goes out of bounds. Sometimes you miss a mark. The temptation is to look at the referee. Or blame the turf. Or yell at the girl who gave you the bad pass. Julie didn't do that. She raised her hand. "My bad." James 5:16 says confession brings healing. In sports, owning your mistake stops the bleeding. It kills the drama. When you say "My fault," you take the pressure off everyone else. The coach respects it. The team trusts it. It allows everyone to reset instantly. Do not waste energy making excuses. Excuses make you look weak. Taking responsibility makes you look strong. Own it, fix it, and dominate the next play. That is the mark of a true captain and a disciplined athlete.

Prayer:

God, keep me humble. When I make a mistake, help me own it and move on. Amen.

Practice:

The next time you make an error, immediately raise your hand and say "My bad." Then hustle.

70
RESPECT THE TWELFTH PLAYER

"On the contrary, those parts of the body that seem to be weaker are indispensable." (1 Corinthians 12:22)

Maya Moore is one of the greatest basketball players ever. She won at UConn, in the WNBA, and the Olympics. She was the star. But she treated the last player on the bench with the same respect as the head coach. 1 Corinthians 12 describes the body of Christ. Every part matters. The toe matters as much as the eye. In sports, the starters get the glory, but the practice squad makes them better. The "weak" players push the starters in drills. Without them, the team is not ready. Maya knew that she needed every single girl in that gym to win a championship. Do not look down on the players who get less playing time. Do not ignore them. High-five them. Encourage them. Value them. They are indispensable. When you respect the whole roster, you build a family that fights for each other. Your character is judged by how you treat those who can't help your stats.

Prayer:

Jesus, thank You for every teammate. Help me treat everyone with equal respect and love. Amen.

Practice:

Find a player who doesn't start or play much. Tell them you appreciate their hard work.

71
KEEP THE LOCKER ROOM CLEAN

"Do not let any unwholesome talk come out of your mouths, but only what is helpful for building others up according to their needs, that it may benefit those who listen." (Ephesians 4:29)

Lolo Jones is a world-class hurdler and bobsledder. She is also open about her faith and her choice to stay pure. Locker rooms can be weird places. Sometimes the music is raunchy. Sometimes the conversation gets dirty or crude. It is considered "cool" to join in. Lolo decided to be different. Ephesians 4:29 sets a high standard: no unwholesome talk. Words have power. Filthy language lowers the standard of the team. It invites the wrong spirit. Lolo didn't preach at people, but she didn't participate. She kept her headphones on or changed the subject. You don't have to be a prude, but you are called to be set apart. Be the one who brings class to the locker room. Keep your speech clean. Keep your music positive. When you respect yourself and your ears, you keep your focus sharp for the race. You can be cool without compromising your values.

Prayer:

Lord, purify my lips and my heart. Help me stand for what is right, even in private. Amen.

Practice:

Check your playlist. Is the music you listen to pre-game building you up or tearing you down?

72

BE THE TEAM GLUE

"Blessed are the peacemakers, for they will be called children of God." (Matthew 5:9)

The USWNT is full of big personalities. Stars everywhere. Egos can clash. Lauren Holiday wasn't the loudest player, but she was the most important. She was the glue. She played in the middle, connecting the defense to the offense. Off the field, she connected people too. She smoothed out drama. Matthew 5 calls peacemakers "blessed." Peace doesn't just happen; you have to make it. Drama destroys seasons faster than bad coaching. When cliques start to form, the Peacemaker bridges the gap. When tempers flare, the Peacemaker brings calm. Lauren Holiday made the team work because she didn't care about credit; she cared about unity. Be the glue. Be the one who holds the group together when things get shaky. A team that stays together is a team that wins championships. Your ability to create peace is a superpower that leads to victory.

Prayer:

Father, make me an instrument of Your peace. Let me bring unity to my team today. Amen.

Practice:

Identify two teammates who don't get along. Try to get them to high-five or talk during warmups.

CHAPTER 6: CHARACTER UNDER PRESSURE

73
FLOPPING IS LYING

"The Lord detests lying lips, but he delights in people who are trustworthy." (Proverbs 12:22)

The crowd screams as the paint gets crowded. Elbows fly. Bodies collide. In the heat of the moment, it would be so easy to snap your head back, flail your arms, and fall to the hardwood to draw the foul. But Tamika Catchings, one of the greatest WNBA players in history, stood her ground. Playing with hearing aids and a fierce work ethic, she battled for every rebound honestly. She knew that flopping is a lie told with your body. It is an attempt to steal a point you did not actually earn. Tamika built her legacy on relentless, honest hustle, wanting to beat opponents because she outworked them, not because she tricked the referee. When you fake a fall in soccer or basketball, you might get the call, but you sacrifice your integrity. You tell yourself that the game is more important than the truth. But God calls you to be trustworthy in the big moments and the split seconds. Your character is a muscle, just like your legs. Win with strength, not deception. Stand tall even when others fall on purpose.

Prayer:

Lord, keep my game honest. Help me win through hard work and skill, never through tricks or lies. Amen.

Practice:

Commit to staying on your feet during contact in your next game or practice. Play through it.

74

THE REF DIDN'T SEE IT

"The eyes of the Lord are everywhere, keeping watch on the wicked and the good." (Proverbs 15:3)

The umpire blinked. The pitch was clearly outside—a ball by three inches—but the umpire called it a strike. The batter groaned in disbelief. Cat Osterman, a softball legend with a spinning left arm, caught the ball back. It is tempting in those moments to smile and think you got away with one. Or worse, to scuff the ball when no one is looking to get more spin. Cat dominated the mound with pure skill and focus, knowing that while umpires miss calls, God never misses a moment. Integrity is how you act when the whistle doesn't blow. It is admitting you touched the ball before it went out of bounds. It is swinging honestly even if the ref has a loose zone. You are not playing for the person in the striped shirt; you are playing for an Audience of One. When you play clean, you sleep well. Your confidence comes from knowing your talent is real, not accidental. Don't settle for a cheap win. Let your game be transparent, because the true Judge sees every play.

Prayer:

Father, remind me that You see everything. Let my character shine brighter than the scoreboard, even when no one watches. Amen.

Practice:

If a ref or coach makes a mistake in your favor during practice, admit it. Be honest immediately.

75

RESPECTING THE ENEMY

"Show proper respect to everyone, love the family of believers, fear God, honor the emperor." (1 Peter 2:17)

The match point ends. The tension snaps. Usually, the loser hangs their head in shame and the winner screams at the sky in triumph. But look at the net. Shelby Rogers, an American tennis star, approaches her opponent not with arrogance, but with a genuine smile. In a sport that is lonely and brutal, Shelby chooses grace. She understands that the girl on the other side of the net is not a villain to be destroyed. She is a fellow creation of God pushing Shelby to be her best. Without a strong opponent, you cannot play a great game. Respecting your enemy means battling them fiercely during the point and honoring them deeply after it. It is refusing to trash talk. It is helping them up if they fall. When you treat opponents with dignity, you show that your identity is built on Christ, not just on the scoreboard. You turn a fierce competition into an opportunity to show the world what love looks like. Be the player who battles hard, but loves harder.

Prayer:

God, help me see my opponents as people made in Your image. Let me compete hard but love harder. Amen.

Practice:

Find one thing you genuinely admire about your rival's game and tell them after the match.

76
WATCH YOUR MOUTH

"May these words of my mouth and this meditation of my heart be pleasing in your sight, Lord, my Rock and my Redeemer." (Psalm 19:14)

Your foot clips the hurdle. Your shin slams into the hard plastic. You hit the track, skin burning against the synthetic surface. The pain is instant and sharp. The first thing that wants to fly out of your mouth is a curse word. Sydney McLaughlin-Levrone knows this pain. As the world record holder in the 400m hurdles, she pushes her body to the breaking point. Yet, she chooses to let her words bring life, not filth. She knows that what comes out in moments of sudden pain reveals what is truly inside your heart. Swearing at the ref, your teammates, or the equipment feels like a release, but it is actually a leak in your character. It shows a lack of self-control. If you can't control your tongue, how can you control your performance? Keep your language holy, even when the sweat stings your eyes. Being a champion means controlling your mouth just as well as you control the ball. Speak life, even when it hurts. Let your reaction be as disciplined as your training.

Prayer:

Lord, guard my tongue. When I am frustrated or in pain, let my words honor You and encourage others. Amen.

Practice:

Pick a clean "power phrase" to say when you mess up, like "Next play" or "Shake it off."

77

CUTTING CORNERS IN PRACTICE

"Whoever walks in integrity walks securely, but whoever takes crooked paths will be found out." (Proverbs 10:9)

The coach blows the whistle. "Run through the line!" he yells. Your lungs are burning. Your legs feel like lead. It is so tempting to slow down three steps before the finish line. Nobody is really watching, right? Allyson Felix, the most decorated track athlete in history, ran thousands of reps. She became a legend because she did not cheat the distance. She knew that cutting a corner in practice creates a hole in your performance. If you cheat the drill, you cheat yourself. You build a habit of quitting right before the breakthrough. Integrity is finishing the sprint when the coach turns his back. It is touching the line on the suicide drill every single time. Those invisible inches add up to gold medals. Do not build your house on crooked paths. Run the full race. Do the full rep. Build a foundation that will hold up when the pressure comes. The security of knowing you did the work is the best armor you can wear on game day. Don't leave your best effort in the shadows.

Prayer:

Jesus, give me the strength to finish strong. Help me do the work right, even when it is hard. Amen.

Practice:

Today, touch every line. Do every rep. If you cheat a rep, do it over immediately.

78

NO EXCUSES, PERIOD

"Whoever conceals their sins does not prosper, but the one who confesses and renounces them finds mercy." (Proverbs 28:13)

The scoreboard shows a loss. The locker room is quiet. It is easy to say the ref was bad, the floor was slippery, or your teammate missed the pass. Dawn Staley, a Hall of Fame player and championship coach, does not tolerate that. She demands accountability. A champion looks in the mirror first. Making excuses is a way to hide your mistakes, and you cannot fix what you hide. If you were late on defense, own it. If you missed the serve, say it. Owning your mess is the only way to clean it up. When you stop making excuses, you start making progress. It takes courage to say "my bad," but that humility attracts mercy and growth. Your coaches will respect you more, and your teammates will trust you deeper. Be the player who takes responsibility, not the one who takes the easy way out. Excuses are the exit ramp on the road to greatness. Stay on the road, confess the error, fix the form, and get better today.

Prayer:

God, help me own my mistakes. Remove my pride so I can learn, grow, and become the teammate I need to be. Amen.

Practice:

Next time you mess up in a game or practice, say "My bad, I will fix it" and move on.

79
CLEANING UP OUR TRASH

"Do everything without grumbling or arguing, so that you may become blameless and pure..." (Philippians 2:14-15)

The ball deflects off the block, spinning wildly toward the back row. It is an ugly play. It is not glorious. But Nyeme, a fierce Libero, dives. She scrapes her elbows and knees to dig a ball that wasn't even her fault. In volleyball, the Libero wears a different jersey and does the dirty work. They clean up the trash. They fix the broken plays so the hitters can shine. This is a spiritual superpower. It is easy to complain when a teammate makes a bad pass. It is hard to hustle and save it without grumbling. Be the player who cleans up the mess. Don't roll your eyes when things go wrong; dive on the floor to make them right. You shine like a star in the universe when you serve others in the gritty, unglamorous moments. Your hustle covers a multitude of errors. Love your team enough to bruise your knees for them. Real leadership isn't just scoring points; it's making everyone around you look better by doing the hard work.

Prayer:

Lord, teach me to serve without complaining. Let me be the one who dives to fix mistakes and lifts others up. Amen.

Practice:

Identify the "trash" tasks on your team (carrying equipment, cleaning up) and do one today without being asked.

80

THINK BEFORE YOU POST

"Set a guard over my mouth, Lord; keep watch over the door of my lips." (Psalm 141:3)

The notification pops up. Someone commented on your photo saying you looked slow or played bad. The anger flares up instantly. Your thumbs hover over the screen, ready to type a nasty comeback. Lolo Jones knows this trap. As an Olympian in hurdles and bobsled, she faced massive online criticism. She learned that clapping back often causes more pain than the original insult. Social media is a minefield. One emotional post can ruin your reputation and hurt your witness. The Holy Spirit is your filter. Before you hit send, ask yourself if that comment builds up or tears down. Silence is often stronger than a snarky reply. Your worth is not found in likes, views, or comments. It is found in Christ. Protect your heart by guarding your digital door. Do not let the world bait you into a fight that does not matter. Use your platform to encourage, not to engage in battles that leave everyone wounded. Let your pause be your power.

Prayer:

Father, control my fingers and my heart. Help me find my worth in You, not in social media approval. Amen.

Practice:

Before you post or comment today, wait five minutes. Ask God if it reflects His love. If not, delete it.

81
THE POST-GAME HANDSHAKE

"Be devoted to one another in love. Honor one another above yourselves."
(Romans 12:10)

The final point is scored. You lost. Your heart is pounding with frustration. You want to smash your racket or storm off the court. But you walk to the net. Coco Gauff, a tennis prodigy, displays maturity beyond her years in these moments. Whether she wins a Grand Slam or loses a heartbreaker, her handshake is firm and her eyes meet her opponent's. The handshake is the ultimate test of character. It says that the relationship is bigger than the result. It is an act of worship to honor the person you just battled. It kills your pride and feeds your spirit. Do not give a limp hand or look away. Look them in the eye and say "good match." It reminds you that you are an athlete of God first. Your grace in defeat screams louder than your celebration in victory. How you handle the loss tells the world who you serve. Honor the game, honor the opponent, and honor God by holding your head high and showing love.

Prayer:

Jesus, give me a graceful heart. Help me honor my opponents whether I win or lose. Let me reflect You at the net. Amen.

Practice:

Make your next post-game handshake the best one yet. Look them in the eye, smile, and mean it.

82

FAKING AN INJURY

"Therefore each of you must put off falsehood and speak truthfully to your neighbor, for we are all members of one body." (Ephesians 4:25)

The tackle was hard, but nothing is broken. You are tired. You want a break. You could stay down, roll around, and wait for the trainer. It would stop the clock. Julie Ertz, a warrior for the US Women's National Team, does not play that way. She is known for grit, often playing with a bandage on her head or bruises on her legs. She gets up. Faking an injury is a form of lying. It disrespects the game, the fans, and the players who are actually hurt. True toughness is getting back on your feet when you want to quit. It is refusing to manipulate the referee for a cheap advantage. God calls us to put off falsehood. Be the player who bounces back up. Show your team that you are resilient. Let your strength be real, not a performance. When you fake it, you weaken your spirit. When you rise, you strengthen your soul. Play the game with honor, knowing that your resilience inspires everyone watching.

Prayer:

God, give me true toughness. Help me stand up when I am knocked down and play with total honesty. Amen.

Practice:

If you fall down in practice today, try to get back up faster than you ever have before.

83
SHORTCUTS DON'T WORK

"The plans of the diligent lead to profit, as surely as haste leads to poverty." (Proverbs 21:5)

You want the perfect curveball today. You want the starting spot now. It is tempting to skip the boring drills and just try to throw hard. Jennie Finch, one of the greatest softball pitchers ever, spent hours just snapping her wrist. She did the small, boring mechanics over and over in the backyard. She knew there are no shortcuts to greatness. Haste leads to poverty— poor form, poor skills, and injury. The shortcut looks faster, but it is a dead end. The long road of diligence is actually the fastest way to your dreams. Do not skip the warm-up. Do not skip the cool-down. Do not skip the fundamental drills. Build your game brick by brick. When the big moment comes, you won't crack because your foundation is solid. Trust the process and do the work that no one sees. The champions you admire didn't get there by magic; they got there by monotony. Embrace the boring work, because that is where the magic is actually made.

Prayer:

Lord, slow me down. Help me love the process and the hard work. Keep me from looking for easy ways out. Amen.

Practice:

Pick the most boring drill for your sport. Do it for 10 minutes today with perfect focus.

84
QUITTING IS TOO EASY

"Let us not become weary in doing good, for at the proper time we will reap a harvest if we do not give up." (Galatians 6:9)

The shark took her arm. The water turned red. Bethany Hamilton lost 60% of her blood and her left arm. It would have been the most logical thing in the world to never touch a surfboard again. Quitting would have been easy. Everyone would have understood. But Bethany got back in the water. She had to relearn everything. She fell thousands of times. She swallowed saltwater and pride. But she did not give up. Now, she surfs massive waves and inspires millions. You will have days where you want to quit. The season is long. The coach is mean. The injury hurts. That is the moment the harvest is growing. Do not grow weary. The breakthrough is often just one more rep away. Grit is refusing to let a bad day turn into a bad life. Stay in the water. Paddle back out. The "harvest" isn't just the win; it's the person you become by refusing to stop. Your perseverance is a testimony that shouts louder than any trophy.

Prayer:

Father, when I am tired and want to quit, renew my strength. Remind me that You are with me in the struggle. Amen.

Practice:

Write "Galatians 6:9" on your wrist or shoe. Look at it when you feel like giving up during practice.

85

WHO AM I AT HOME?

"Even small children are known by their actions, so is their conduct really pure and upright?" (Proverbs 20:11)

The cameras flash. The gold medal shines. On TV, Shawn Johnson East looked like the perfect American sweetheart. But she had to ask herself: Who am I when the cameras turn off? It is easy to be kind when fans are watching. It is harder to be kind to your parents when you are tired and hungry in your own kitchen. Your character is not defined by your highlight reel. It is defined by how you treat your siblings, your parents, and your friends in private. God sees the heart. He wants you to be the same person in the dark as you are in the light. Do not be a fake champion. Be a real one. Let your conduct be pure at the dinner table, not just on the podium. Real integrity is consistent kindness. If you are a hero to the world but a villain at home, you have missed the point. Bring your championship attitude into your living room and serve your family with love.

Prayer:

Jesus, help me be the same person everywhere I go. Let me show love to my family just as much as my teammates. Amen.

Practice:

Do one specific chore at home today without being asked, just to serve your family.

86

THE HARD RIGHT CHOICE

"...choose for yourselves this day whom you will serve... But as for me and my household, we will serve the Lord." (Joshua 24:15)

The offer was massive. Playboy magazine offered Jennie Finch a huge stack of money to pose for them. She was young, famous, and could have used the cash. The world said, "Do it, you're beautiful!" But Jennie said no. She chose the hard right over the easy wrong. She knew that her body and her witness were more valuable than a paycheck. She wanted to be a role model for girls like you, not an object for men. Every day you face choices. Go to the party or go to practice? Cheat on the test or take the C? Join the gossip or walk away? Joshua drew a line in the sand. You must draw yours. Choose today whom you will serve. The hard choice usually brings the greatest peace. Stand firm in your values, even if it costs you money or popularity. Your "no" to the world creates space for God's "yes" in your life. Be brave enough to be different, and let your choices glorify the King.

Prayer:

Lord, give me the courage to say no to the world and yes to You. Help me choose what is right, not what is easy. Amen.

Practice:

Identify one "easy wrong" you are tempted by (gossip, laziness, cheating) and make a plan to avoid it tomorrow.

Phil 4:13
I can do all things.

CHAPTER 7:
PLAYING FOR GLORY

87

MY JERSEY IS A PULPIT

"For I am not ashamed of the gospel, because it is the power of God that brings salvation to everyone who believes." (Romans 1:16)

The stadium lights blaze like artificial suns, cutting through the night. Sydney McLaughlin-Levrone crosses the finish line, lungs burning and legs heavy, with a new world record flashing on the board. The cameras swarm immediately. A microphone is shoved into her face while she catches her breath. It is the biggest moment of her career, and millions are watching. It would be easy to talk about her training, her speed, or her diet. Instead, Sydney smiles and gives glory to God. She views the track as her mission field. She knows that winning gives her a voice, and she uses that voice to point back to Jesus. You do not need a global TV interview to do this. Your jersey is your pulpit. The way you handle a bad call, the way you encourage a struggling teammate, and the way you play with integrity speaks louder than a sermon. Your teammates are watching your life closely. When you play with love and honor, you show them who Jesus is without saying a single word.

Prayer:

Lord, let my actions on the field point others to You. I want to represent You well today. Amen.

Practice:

Write "For His Glory" on your wrist tape or equipment today. Let it remind you why you play.

88
PRAYING FOR MY OPPONENT

"But I tell you, love your enemies and pray for those who persecute you." (Matthew 5:44)

The sand is scorching hot and the net stands like a wall between enemies. In beach volleyball, the rivalry is personal and fierce. You stare your opponent in the eyes before every serve, looking for weakness. Kelly Cheng wants to win every set she plays. But she does something radical off the sand. She hosts Bible studies and invites the very women she plays against. It sounds backward to help the competition spiritually. But Kelly knows her identity is in Christ, not in beating someone else. When she prays for her opponents, the bitterness of competition melts away. It turns the game from a war into a form of collective worship. You can do this too. That girl on the other team who plays rough? Pray for her. The team that always talks trash? Pray for them. It is impossible to hate someone you are praying for. It frees you to play your best game without the heavy weight of anger dragging you down or clouding your focus.

Prayer:

Jesus, help me see my opponents as people You love. Guard my heart against anger and bitterness. Amen.

Practice:

Pick one rival player or team today. Pray for their safety and health before the game starts.

89
WHY I WRITE ON MY SHOE

"Tie them as symbols on your hands and bind them on your foreheads. Write them on the doorframes of your houses and on your gates." (Deuteronomy 6:8-9)

The laces are tight. The court surface is pristine. Coco Gauff sits on the sideline during a changeover, wiping sweat from her forehead. The pressure in a tennis match is isolating because you are out there all alone with your thoughts. But Coco looks down at her shoes. Written in marker are words of faith. It is a visual anchor. When the score is down and the crowd is loud, a quick glance at her feet reminds her of the truth. She is not just playing for a trophy; she is playing under God's care. You need visual reminders too. Your mind will drift toward fear or insecurity during a game. You need truth to pull you back. Writing a verse on your shoe, your wrist, or keeping a sticky note in your gym bag acts like a spiritual anchor. It stops the drift. It reminds you that God is with you in every set, every quarter, and every difficult moment.

Prayer:

God, keep Your truth in front of my eyes. Remind me that You are with me when I forget. Amen.

Practice:

Use a sharpie or tape to put a scripture reference or cross on your gear where you can see it.

90

THANK YOU FOR MY LEGS

"For you created my inmost being; you knit me together in my mother's womb." (Psalm 139:13)

The snow flies up in a cold, white spray. Amy Purdy carves down the mountain on a snowboard, moving with power, speed, and grace. But if you look closely, you see her legs are made of carbon fiber and metal. Amy lost her legs to meningitis, but she did not lose her spirit. She became a Paralympian who thanks God for the body she has, even with its differences. She focuses entirely on what her body can do, not what it cannot do. It is easy to stand in front of a mirror and criticize your thighs, your height, or your arms. Stop that immediately. Your body is a miraculous instrument designed by God to move, run, and jump. Gratitude turns what you have into enough. When you thank God for your strong lungs and working muscles, you stop comparing yourself to others and start playing with freedom. Your body is a gift, so treat it with the respect a masterpiece deserves.

Prayer:

Father, thank You for this body. Help me treat it with respect and use it to honor You. Amen.

Practice:

List three physical things you are thankful for about your body (strong arms, good balance, health).

91

SENIOR NIGHT SADNESS

"He has made everything beautiful in its time." (Ecclesiastes 3:11)

The final buzzer sounds. The crowd stands to cheer, but your heart feels heavy. Carli Lloyd played her final soccer game for the US National Team knowing it was the end of an era. She unlaced her cleats and walked off the field she dominated for years. Leaving a sport or moving on from a team is heartbreaking. It feels like losing a part of yourself. Whether it is graduating high school or changing clubs, transitions are scary. But God designs life in seasons. Just as winter turns to spring, one chapter ends so a new one can begin. Carli trusted that her identity was not just "soccer player." You are more than your jersey number. If you are facing a transition, know that God is already in your tomorrow. The sadness is real, but so is the hope. He is making the next season beautiful too. You do not have to cling to the past to find happiness; God has fresh joy waiting for you ahead.

Prayer:

Lord, I trust You with my future. Thank You for the past season, and lead me into the new one. Amen.

Practice:

Write down one favorite memory from this season and one thing you are excited about for the next one.

92

PLAYING HARD IS WORSHIP

"Therefore, I urge you, brothers and sisters, in view of God's mercy, to offer your bodies as a living sacrifice, holy and pleasing to God—this is your true and proper worship." (Romans 12:1)

The gun cracks through the silent air. Athing Mu takes off in the 800-meter run. Her stride is long, powerful, and elegant. She does not run tentatively. She runs with everything she has. For Athing, the track is not just a place to compete; it is a place to offer a sacrifice of effort. Playing hard is a spiritual act. When you dive for a loose ball, sprint through the line, or hold a squat until your legs shake, you are telling God, "Thank you for this talent." Laziness insults the Giver of the gift. Maximum effort honors Him. Do not hold back today. Do not save energy for later. Pour it all out. Let your sweat be your offering. When you play with that kind of intensity, you are not just an athlete; you are a worshiper in motion. God is glorified when you use the gifts He gave you to their absolute limit, refusing to coast or settle for average.

Prayer:

God, I give You my full effort today. I will not be lazy. Let my hard work be my worship. Amen.

Practice:

Pick one drill today where you usually slack off. Go 100% intensity on it as an offering to God.

93

PRAYING FOR MY COACH

"I urge, then, first of all, that petitions, prayers, intercession and thanksgiving be made for all people—for kings and all those in authority..." (1 Timothy 2:1-2)

The timeout huddle is tense. Coach is drawing up a play, voice hoarse, forehead sweating. Dawn Staley is a legendary coach, but she bears a heavy burden. She is responsible for wins, losses, the media, and the hearts of her players. She needs prayer just as much as the rookie on the bench. It is easy to get frustrated with your coach when they yell, run you hard, or bench you. But have you ever stopped to pray for them? They are human. They have stress, families, and fears. When you pray for your coach, your heart toward them softens. You start to see them with compassion rather than annoyance. Ask God to give them wisdom and patience. A team that prays for their leader is a team that stays united. Be the player who blesses the coach, not the one who complains about them in the locker room. Your prayers can change the atmosphere of the entire team.

Prayer:

Lord, bless my coach today. Give them wisdom, patience, and peace. Help me to respect and learn from them. Amen.

Practice:

Say a silent 5-second prayer for your coach while they are talking or running practice today.

94

WHAT WILL THEY REMEMBER?

"A good name is more desirable than great riches; to be esteemed is better than silver or gold." (Proverbs 22:1)

The stats sheet is full of numbers. Points, rebounds, steals. But when Tamika Catchings retired from basketball, people did not just talk about her stats. They talked about her heart. They talked about her foundation "Catch the Stars" and how she encouraged kids. She built a good name, not just a good record. Medals eventually get put in a drawer. Trophies collect dust. But the way you made people feel lasts forever. Think about your team right now. When you graduate, what will they say about you? Will they say you were a ball hog who only cared about scoring? Or will they say you were kind, hard-working, and a great teammate? Build a legacy of love. Be the player who helps the freshman up. Be the one who cheers the loudest for the last player on the bench. That is the reputation that matters. Your character will outlast your career, so build it with as much focus as you build your skills.

Prayer:

Jesus, help me build a good name. Let me be remembered for my kindness and character, not just my skill. Amen.

Practice:

Compliment a teammate today on something that has nothing to do with their performance, like their attitude.

95
LIFE AFTER THE BUZZER

"For I know the plans I have for you," declares the Lord, "plans to prosper you and not to harm you, plans to give you hope and a future." (Jeremiah 29:11)

The stadium is empty. The locker room is quiet. Lauren Holiday was at the top of the soccer world, but she stepped away. Injuries happen. Retirement comes. Sometimes life forces you out of the game before you are ready. It feels like the world is ending when you cannot play the sport you love. But your sport is what you do, not who you are. Lauren knew God had plans for her as a wife, mom, and advocate that were just as important as scoring goals. If you are injured or sitting on the bench, do not despair. God's plan for your life is bigger than a court or a field. He is writing a story that includes your sport but goes far beyond it. Trust the Author. He knows exactly what He is doing with your future. You are not defined by your stats; you are defined by His love, and that never retires or fades away.

Prayer:

Father, I trust Your plans. Even when I cannot play or things change, I know You are holding my future. Amen.

Practice:

Write down two things you love doing or are good at outside of your sport.

96

FEELING GOD'S PLEASURE

"Let them praise his name with dancing and make music to him with timbrel and harp. For the Lord takes delight in his people." (Psalm 149:3-4)

The wind rushes past your ears. Your legs pump in a rhythm that feels like music. Sydney McLaughlin-Levrone describes running as feeling God's pleasure. It is that "Chariots of Fire" moment where the effort does not feel like work; it feels like flying. God designed you to move. He gave you those fast-twitch muscle fibers. He gave you that coordination. When you use those gifts with joy, God smiles. He delights in watching you play. Too often, we play with fear of messing up. We play stiff and worried. But God wants you to play with freedom. He loves to see you run, jump, and compete. Next time you are in the middle of the action, take a split second to feel the joy of it. You were made for this. Run like Heaven is cheering you on. Let the pressure fall away and just enjoy the ability to move. When you enjoy the game, you glorify the Creator who made you.

Prayer:

Lord, thank You for the gift of sport. Help me to feel Your pleasure and joy when I compete. Amen.

Practice:

Smile during your warm-up today. Remind yourself that this is fun and God loves watching you.

97

HELPING THE ROOKIE

"Then they can urge the younger women..." (Titus 2:4)

The halfpipe looks like an icy monster. Standing at the top, knees can shake. Kelly Clark was the queen of snowboarding for years. She saw a young teenager named Chloe Kim coming up the ranks. Chloe was good—good enough to beat Kelly. Instead of being cold or competitive, Kelly mentored her. She poured wisdom into the rookie. She knew that a true champion builds the next generation. It is easy to feel threatened by the younger girl who is fast and talented. Do not be. Be the leader who welcomes her. Show her the ropes. Encourage her when she fails. There is enough room in God's kingdom for both of you to shine. When you help a rookie, you show confidence in who God made you to be. Security creates kindness; insecurity creates meanness. Be secure. Your legacy isn't just what you win, but who you help along the way. Be the senior who makes the freshman feel like they belong.

Prayer:

Jesus, help me to be a leader. Show me a younger or newer player I can encourage and help today. Amen.

Practice:

Identify the newest or youngest girl on your team. High-five her and tell her "good job" at practice.

98

SPORTS SPEAK ALL LANGUAGES

"Their voice goes out into all the earth, their words to the ends of the world." (Psalm 19:4)

A basketball bounces with the same rhythm in New York as it does in Beijing. A soccer goal brings the same cheer in Brazil as it does in England. Maya Moore understood that sport is a universal language. She used her platform not just to sell shoes, but to speak out for justice. She stepped away from the WNBA to fight for a man wrongly imprisoned. She knew her influence could change lives. You have that same language. You can use your sport to connect with kids who do not look like you or speak your language. You can use your position to stand up for what is right at your school. Sport breaks down barriers. It opens doors. Walk through them with the love of Jesus. Do not just play the game; use the game to make a difference in your world. Your athletic talent is a key that unlocks doors to people's hearts—make sure you walk through them with a message of love.

Prayer:

Lord, use my sport to connect with others. Give me the courage to stand for what is right. Amen.

Practice:

Invite someone who is not in your usual friend group to join in a game or drill this week.

99

PLAYING WITH JOY AGAIN

"Do not grieve, for the joy of the Lord is your strength." (Nehemiah 8:10)

The heavy shot put lands with a thud. The measurement confirms it: Gold Medal. The stadium in Paris erupts. Yemisi Ogunleye is overcome with emotion. But she does not just wave. She grabs a microphone and sings. In front of the whole world, she belts out a gospel song about God's faithfulness. It was a moment of pure, unashamed joy. Sometimes the pressure to perform steals our happiness. We worry so much about the outcome that we forget to love the moment. Yemisi reminded us that the joy of the Lord is stronger than the pressure of the Olympics. If you have lost your spark, go back to the source. God is your strength. When you play with His joy in your heart, the pressure fades, and the game becomes beautiful again. Sing in your heart and let it fly. Do not let the stress of the scoreboard steal the song in your heart. You play best when your spirit is light.

Prayer:

God, restore my joy. Take away the heavy pressure and let me play with a light and happy heart. Amen.

Practice:

Sing a worship song in the car or on the bus on the way to your game or practice.

100
THE CROWN THAT LASTS

"Everyone who competes in the games goes into strict training. They do it to get a crown that will not last, but we do it to get a crown that will last forever." (1 Corinthians 9:25)

The gold medal is heavy and cool to the touch. It shines under the lights. Allyson Felix has more medals than almost any track athlete in history. But she knows a secret. Eventually, medals tarnish. Records are broken. People forget who won the championship ten years ago. Allyson runs for a prize that does not fade. She runs to hear "Well done, good and faithful servant" from Jesus. It is okay to want to win. Work hard for that trophy. But remember it is just metal. The real prize is who you become in the process. The discipline, the faith, and the character you build—those are the crowns that last forever. When you focus on the eternal prize, losing a game does not crush you, and winning a game does not puff you up. You are chasing something better. Let your sport be the tool God uses to shape your soul for eternity, not just your body for a season.

Prayer:

Lord, help me keep my eyes on the real prize. I want a faith that lasts longer than any trophy. Amen.

Practice:

Look at a trophy or ribbon you won. Remind yourself, "This is nice, but Jesus is better."

101

I GIVE YOU THIS GAME

"Commit to the Lord whatever you do, and he will establish your plans." (Proverbs 16:3)

The air is thick with chalk dust. The vault runway stretches out ahead. Simone Biles takes a deep breath. The world is watching, waiting for a mistake. But before she raises her hand to salute the judges, she often whispers a prayer. She commits the routine to God. It is an act of surrender. She is saying, "Lord, I have done the work, now the results are Yours." That is the secret to mental toughness. When you try to control everything, you get tight and anxious. When you hand the game over to God, you get freedom. You can trust Him with the win, and you can trust Him with the loss. Before you step onto the court or field today, visualize yourself handing the ball to Jesus. It is His game. Go play it with His power. Release the heavy burden of perfectionism and trade it for the peace of trusting God. He has got you, so go fly.

Prayer:

Jesus, I give this game to You. I trust You with the results. Help me play freely and boldly. Amen.

Practice:

Right before the whistle blows or the game starts, whisper, "Lord, I give this to You."

KEEP GOING

The gym is quiet again.

Your ponytail is a little messy and your jersey is soaked with sweat. Your heartbeat is finally slowing down, but your spirit feels wide awake. You can feel it, can't you? You are different than you were on day one.

You made it. You finished every story, every verse, and every challenge that asked you to grow stronger inside and out. That is something to celebrate with a huge high-five. You kept showing up for yourself and for God. You learned how to stay calm when the pressure hit. You built heart habits that will follow you everywhere.

You prayed before you scrolled through your phone. You practiced your drills when no one was watching. You found peace when everyone else felt like they were in a panic. You learned that playing your sport can actually be a way to worship Jesus. That is what real championship living looks like.

You are now part of a special group of girls who know that faith is the secret to the grind. Sydney McLaughlin-Levrone does it before she ever touches a hurdle. Simone Biles does it when the whole world is watching her every move. Coco Gauff does it by dropping to her knees in prayer on the court. And now, you are doing it too.

But here is the twist. The world outside this book can still be loud.

Tomorrow, a teammate might be mean. You might get a grade you do not like. You might have a practice where everything feels heavy and hard. In those moments, it is easy to forget that you are a daughter of the King. It is easy to think your worth is back on the scoreboard.

That is why you have to keep going.

Champions are not perfect. They just never stop returning to the truth. When you mess up or miss a day, you do not lose your progress. You just get a fresh start from a God who loves you more than any trophy. That is what faith feels like. It is a safety net that catches you every single time.

When you walk out of this book, take these lessons with you. Bring them into the classroom, the locker room, and the hallways at school. Remember that God is training you in every space, not just when you are reading your Bible. The same peace that steadied your heart during these pages can show up when the crowd is screaming or when a test feels impossible.

If you ever feel stuck, come back to a page that made you smile. Read it again. Whisper the prayer one more time. The same God who met you here is still listening. He never stops coaching you. He never stops believing in you.

This is not the end of your story. It is just the beginning of your best season yet.

You have built a foundation that will keep growing. You have learned to trust, to focus, and to breathe when things get tough. I have so much more waiting for you too. Keep your eyes open for more stories and new ways to grow your game and your faith at the same time. There are always new verses to learn and new "reps" to add to your spiritual training plan.

Until then, stay ready. Keep praying first. Keep showing up early. Keep finishing strong. Your life is the arena now. Your mindset is your gear. Your faith is your superpower.

God called you to be a champion. You already are one.

Now go live like it.

Your feedback is a true blessing!

If this book has encouraged you or helped you feel less alone, would you leave a quick review?

Even one sentence makes a huge difference and takes just a minute. As a small author, your feedback not only lifts my heart... it also helps other women of faith with find the support and hope they need.

Thank you for being part of this journey!

Scan this QR code with your phone to go to the review page

Or

Go to your orders, find the book and click

"Write a product review"

Thank you <3

If you liked this book, you can check out my other books as well:

Scan the QR to see my books on my author page!

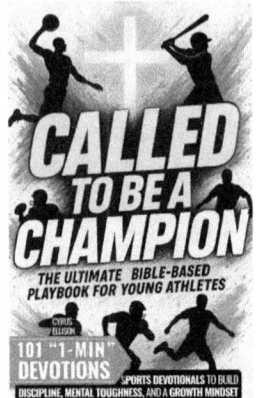

www.ingramcontent.com/pod-product-compliance
Lightning Source LLC
Chambersburg PA
CBHW071520120626
46550CB00006B/2289